The Quantum Children

A Parent's Guide for the 21st Century

Book 1

Michael Orwig

Be in Joy

Michael Orwig 9/14/17

The Quantum Children: A Parent's Guide for the 21st Century
Book 1

To learn more about Michael Orwig's work, please contact him through his website: *www.thequantumchildrenbook.com*

Library of Congress Cataloging-in-Publication Data

Author Name, Michael D. Orwig, MS
Title, The Quantum Children: A Parent's Guide for the 21st Century
Book 1

ISBN: #978-1-5136-1310-9 (Paperback)

ISBN: # 978-1-5136-1311-6 (eBook)

1. Family and Relationships/ Parenting/ General   2. Social Science/ Children's Studies   3. Family and Relationships/ Children with special needs

First edition, October 2016
Cover Design by Empowered Whole Being Press

Empowered Whole Being Press
www.EmpoweredWholeBeingPress.com

In 2002 I met Lesley Michaels. She is one of the best spirit channels that you will find anywhere. At that time, she was working with Jesus and Mary Magdalene creating a series of channeled messages that became a three year class known as "The Apprenticeship to Awakening Divinity." Over the years, I have continued my relationship with Lesley and have more than one hundred and fifty hours of material. In 2008, when I began working on this book (this is its fourth writing), I asked Jesus and Mary if they would give a special message to the parents. Here is that message. (Jeshua and Jesus are the same.)

Message from Jeshua and Mary to the Parents

Greetings to you all.

We welcome you to these new levels of understanding of all that is transpiring in your world, including the great shifts in the way that the dear souls of this universe are entering the planet in order to have their greater effects on humanity, the planet itself, and the universe. We honor you for being the ones to bring forward onto the planet these great souls who are entering with advanced wisdom and awareness of who they are and what they are here to accomplish, and certainly it is that within the existence of the relationship between you and these dear ones there is going to be a new paradigm, a new model if you will, that will be created in terms of how to be parents on the physical plane. And all of this will revolve around a more expanded understanding that you will teach each other of how to be models to these souls by being present as oneself.

In the earlier stages of your evolutions, parenting was addressed from a perspective of shaping and molding the young ones. And this was correct as it was the natural stage of evolution within which you found yourselves at these earlier times. Now, however, the approach that is to be offered is to invite these young ones to be in greater sharing of what it is they know...what it is they would like to shape within the reality of physical life and then instead of directing them as to how to accomplish this, being present with them in determining together how it is that these new visions will come to be. Above all, know that this is an exciting adventure. Approach it as such, and as you do those to whom you are guardian will express the same and even greater levels of enthusiasm for the adventure that you will be co-creating together.

Much joy with this, dear ones.

Jeshua and Mary

Image by Sarah Haras (2)

White Tiger Spirit

Seeker of Personal Truth (3)

With Power and Strength, you glide through the night,
silent as the mist that evaporates with
the first rays of morning light

Eyes, glowing with a blue fire that reflects both water and sky,
you stare deeply into the Soul, leaving nothing unknown,
for all is revealed before your penetrating gaze

Keenest of all is the gaze you turn Inward,
searching the depths of your restless spirit
in a quest to know your Self

The Hunt for Personal Truth is called
and swiftly answered

When the Truth is revealed, torn free from the grasp of the past,
any fear felt is faced with stealthy observation
and unrelenting determination,
for Fear now is the Prey

Dedicated

To all of the new children and their beautiful parents

In gratitude

In gratitude to all of the spirit help without whose love, aid, information and guidance this book would have never been written. Mother Mary, Mary Magdalene, the men and women of the Order of Isis, Quan Yin, and my guide throughout the writing, Robert Lewis Stevenson, who aided me in always finding the right word.

To my wife Allyn, who helped me in every area of this book, but especially with her understandings of natural medicine.

And a very special thank you to Lesley Michaels whose additional channeled information has been a blessing on so many levels as this book was composed.

Thank you all

Michael

Table of Contents

Introduction

Who are the Quantum children? It is a question I hear asked all the time and one I will address soon enough.

Yet in reality, we all are Quantum children. Of course, as a book on parenting, this book focuses primarily on helping and supporting our young ones. However, the information conveyed throughout is for everyone. All of humanity is going through an awakening from third density consciousness. It is part of our evolution and the children that are coming onto Earth at this time are a major part of this shift. The problem is, a great deal of society is still working from paradigms tied to the past and do not support these children.

Every structure in society operates from the beliefs and the level of consciousness that created it. The education system is a type of structure. The medical system is another. You could even look at the family unit as a structure. Governments, religions and all of our other industries in our society form structures as well. By their very natures, structures are resistant to change. The motivations behind this resistance may be money, power, politics, or any combination of these. We are living in a time of awakening and great change. Don't look for these structures to be at the forefront of this change. Unfortunately, they are the ball and chain holding us back. It is going to be up to you as a parent or grandparent to shift into the new paradigms our children need and to find alternatives that support you and your family. We are moving into an unknown reality, which can be scary. It doesn't have to be that way though. The main purpose of this book series is to guide you into a new reality.

This book is a compilation of information from many sources. For as long as I can remember, I have enjoyed finding out what was going on behind the scenes of life. As a consequence, this book contains a lot of esoteric information. Years ago, this information would never have been available to the public but the timing is right for the understandings to be introduced to all of society. I have included information from Esther Hicks, my good friend Lesley Michaels, and material from my own meditations. Esther Hicks works with the group entity that she refers to as Abraham. Lesley Michaels works with a lot of different individuals; however, most of her material that is included in this book came from Jeshua (Jesus) and Mary Magdalene. In my meditations I was working directly with the group consciousness of the Quantum children and the light council headed by Mother Mary that supports and oversees them. Certainly, whenever I could bring in scientific understandings, I did. This includes information from both quantum physics and the natural sciences. The perspective of this book is definitely not from that of your average child psychologist.

My job in this process was to take all of this information, regardless of how complex it might be, weave it all together and then write it in a way anyone could understand. Within this task, I tried to connect the dots in such a way that you would have a much fuller understanding of everything going on within these shifts of consciousness.

Many of the topics covered in this book have multiple layers of complexity. It is the nuances and subtleties that need to be experienced in order for us to move our understandings from knowledge to wisdom. Take the concept of "how thoughts create." I look at goal setting as our first level of understanding in this area. Most people, however, don't understand the limitations of goal setting. They feel that if they are determined enough, they can pound away at something until they succeed. So as good as goal setting is, it carries with it an element of force. I consider the Law of Attraction as our second level. This material is excellent but it still isn't the top of the mountain. There is more beyond it. This is true for every topic within this book. Unfortunately, we just can't absorb it all at once. Thusly, I gave you the biggest bite I thought you could handle and the next installment in this series will pick up where this one leaves off. I've also placed a lot of references for you in the latter part of the book. If something interests you, keep exploring.

Hopefully at some point in time as you read this manuscript, I will touch upon information you have never heard before or information that may go against one of your beliefs. I wouldn't be doing my job if this didn't occur. Don't fight with it. The worst thing you can do is get into a right/wrong type of tug of war. One technique that I use in a situation such as this is to just view it as an interesting point of view and move on. If you need to, just set those concepts aside for a period of time and come back to them later. It's okay. Not everything I give you is going to resonate with you immediately. This book is designed to push your boundaries and limitations. It is natural to find resistance in these areas.

Most importantly, have fun with this material.

Section 1:
The Quantum children

1

Changing Paradigms

"It was the best of times. It was the worst of times." Charles Dickens

We are at the end of a great cycle within our evolution and the birth of another. It is a time of Awakening and a time of Change. We all are going through a great metamorphosis and how each person handles the change will determine which side of that famous Dickens' quotation they will be on. Humanity has prepared for this timeframe for thousands of years, and now it is upon us. Humankind is in full transition from the fear that has ruled our existence in the physical universe into a more enlightened age where we are more connected to our higher levels of consciousness and to all that exists around us. Our evolution is accelerating rapidly and our children are here to teach and lead us, as much as we are to teach and lead them. There is greatness in every single person on this planet and yet so many of us still carry thoughts and beliefs that are tethered to structures that are based in fear, lack and limitation.

Each of us has a set of internal structures through which we look at the world. Our asserted identities, our wounds and our personality form the core components of these structures. The problem is, these are not who we are. They are not our true selves. They are illusionary veils that we hide behind. The more we dissolve and let go of these veils, the more we are able to experience the world through the clarity and transparency of love that resides at the core of each one of us.

Our old beliefs, paradigms, and societal structures have been based on lack, competition and control for a very long time. These structures are merely reflections of our internal structures. The new levels that we are moving into are based on cooperation, unconditional love and the letting go of all judgment. The old beliefs reflect our internal disconnection from our "authentic self" and from Source[1]. This separation is dissolving, and as such we are creating a new world. In the meantime, we are living in transition where both levels of thought exist simultaneously. The new children are coming in to help create a new reality, one free of judgment and aggression.

As parents, we are constantly attempting to pass on our beliefs, our morals, and our wisdom to our children. This practice has served us well for thousands of years. The problem with this now is that much of the programming in our minds comes from structures in society that were formed with paradigms and beliefs that no longer serve us. We have lack and limitation versus abundance and limitlessness. We have competition versus cooperation. And most importantly, we have struggle versus joy and happiness. Lack, limitation and competition are all tied to paradigms and beliefs of the past and to various forms of Separation consciousness. It is a level of consciousness that does not see its connection to all that is. Individuals see themselves as hapless victims instead of the magnificent creators they are.

The conditioning of our children does not begin after they are born. It starts from the point of conception and moves through every aspect of the pregnancy. As the cells of the fetus are formed from the mother's body, information is transferred to the child. Everything that is going on with the mother during the pregnancy is passed on and coded into the silicon levels of the child's cells. Obviously, this could be as much a challenge as a blessing, but in either instance it is still a gift that each of us is choosing and accepting. Of the many codes that are passed on to the growing baby while it is in the

---

[1] You will find that I use the word Source instead of God to refer to the creational energy of the universe. I do this for one primary reason. It does not have all of the conditioning from religious dogma that the word God has. The male-dominated church loved to create the image of God in a masculine form, whereas God or Source is all that is, and as such is neither divine masculine nor divine feminine. It is both simultaneously.

mother's womb, the mother's self-image is probably the most important.

As souls, the growing babies are completely aware of everything that is going on with their potential parents. The first order of business that occurs between the soul of the child and that of its prospective parents is the forming of a soul contract. Once that is completed, the child's soul can begin inhabiting the fetus. This soul contract could occur before the pregnancy or it could happen in the ninth month.

Let's say for example that a soul-level contract between the parents and the incoming soul occurs at three months into the mother's pregnancy. The incoming soul can move from the spirit side and begin to inhabit its growing body at that time or it can wait until later. Some incoming souls have even waited until several days after the birth before fully merging with their new bodies. Sometimes, if a soul has not had a physical existence for a long time, he or she may move into the body for brief periods of the pregnancy and then move back to the spirit side. It's like dipping your toe in the water to see what it feels like.

Anything is possible, and we as souls are constantly evaluating the ongoing situation and making choices accordingly. I've often heard the saying from someone referring to his or her challenging parents, "Well we don't choose our parents, only our friends." Nothing could be further from the truth. We absolutely choose our parents — and needless to say, it is a very important choice. Why you chose them is normally not understood until later in your life, but if you really wanted to know, there are techniques in hypnotherapy that can unveil this information for you.

Once a child is born, our effect on them escalates. During early childhood, virtually everything in a child's environment is imprinted at their subconscious level. Psychologists for decades have known that children's brains normally operate in the relaxed brain states of alpha, theta and delta. This is truly our best state of learning. A young child is literally recording and storing information about its environment every moment of the day. This puts into place many of our programs and beliefs about the new environment and can last a lifetime.

As an adult, when we perform a task or have a specific emotion, neural pathways in the brain begin to form. The more a task is performed the stronger these pathways become. Children, however, develop similar neural pathways, not by doing the activity or having the emotion but by observation. In the 1960s, a neurophysiologist from Italy, Dr. Giacoma Rizzolatti and his team of scientists at the University of Parma discovered the existence in the brain of what scientists call mirror neurons. These neurons fire when an individual observes an action or when the action is performed. What scientists have found is that the same neural pathways are activated whether the action is performed physically, observed, or envisioned. Athletic coaches have embraced this concept for decades and have incorporated visualization in all of their training. *For a parent or grandparent, it is important to remember we are constantly modeling for our children.*

Think of the new[2] children as a brand-new computer with the latest and greatest new operating system. Let's call it "Version nine hundred." You, as a parent or grandparent, are constantly introducing into this computer all of your internal programmings. This programming exists as your fears and your joys and how you go through life in general. As energy, it ripples and flows through every cell of your child. Some of these programmings are founded on love and some on separation, and your child absorbs every one of them. The problem is that our programs, rooted in competition, control and judgment literally act like a virus within their system. And what occurs any time you introduce a virus into a computer? Problems, lots of problems. Individual files become corrupted, leading to

---

[2] When I refer to the new children, I am referring to the children born since the year 2000. The Quantum children are not limited to just this age group.

applications shutting down or failing. There's even a possibility of the entire operating system crashing. In short, a mess, and this is what is happening to these new children daily.

The reason I chose the name of the new version of our consciousness as "Version nine hundred" is a simple one. We are constantly evolving. It is happening every minute of every day. I simply chose a fairly large number to illustrate that we have been advancing along an evolutionary spiral for a long time, and calling it version 2.0 would give you the thought that this is the first major shift we have gone through, and that wouldn't be the truth.

Beliefs

Perception is reality

Each of us works our way through reality looking through the rose-colored glasses of our perception. This point of view is based primarily upon our beliefs. To the mind, a belief is nothing more than a thought that we have had over and over. Our *belief* that a particular thought or concept is true is the only thing that is important to the mind. Like a computer, our minds run programs and once a particular concept or thought is accepted as true it is going to continue to run unless something new is introduced to change it. Every single one of us is operating from a compendium of thoughts, some of them true, some partially true, and some that have no truth to them whatsoever. For hundreds of years people believed that the Earth was flat and that the sun revolved around the Earth, and these are just a couple of examples.

We are constantly being conditioned by our environment and our experiences. What frequently isn't taken into account is that our beliefs are creating our experiences. This circle effect is much like the argument about what came first, the chicken or the egg. When it comes to how we create our individual reality, either of these could come first. An experience could create a belief just as readily as a belief could create an experience. Furthermore, once a belief has been created, we will do everything within our power to validate it. Our parents were conditioned to believe that smoking was sexy, looked cool and that there were no health side effects. This image, created by the tobacco industry, thrived within society for more than seventy years.

Not a day goes by that we aren't conditioned in some way. It could come from a parent, a teacher, an advertisement, the media, the government, or a church. The list is infinite. The more you hear a particular thought the more your mind begins to see it as true. Our relationship to these sources is extremely important. The more our minds see any individual or agency as having authority over us, the more we tend to allow their thoughts into our consciousness. Certainly, our relationship with our parents is our strongest in this regard but virtually every authority figure or structure in our society may create strong associations in our minds.

In many ways, our belief structures are products of the information that we have been exposed to and have been given strength and power within our minds. When we recognize that no two individuals on the planet are working with exactly the same information, it is easy to see why there would be such a variance in peoples' points of view. In many ways if there is a difference in two peoples' beliefs, what we are actually saying is that the information each is working with is simply different. Many of the different thoughts and concepts that I will be sharing are based on information that is not common within society. As such, you may have been exposed to some of the information but most likely not. It is not my wish to try to convince you that a particular belief you hold is wrong and that mine is right. I simply wish you to be open to the expansions that I will be offering to you and if something doesn't resonate for you feel free to discard it. The choice is yours, unconditionally.

So, with that in mind, I would like to talk about some core concepts that I work with and how they relate to the information in this book.

1. Everything is Energy
2. Consciousness
3. We are vibrational creatures living in a vibrational universe (Abraham/Hicks)
4. We exist not only as physical bodies but as overlapping fields of energy and information known as morphogenetic fields
5. The children coming to this planet are highly advanced souls, not just children
6. Life is a continuum, not just a single lifetime

Energy

Frequently, you will hear me say throughout this book that "everything is energy." This is more of a quantum view than a physical one. We look around us and everything appears solid. The desk that I am writing on certainly appears solid, but is it really? The answer is, of course, no. As we move into the subatomic realm all of the mass that we thought looked like billiard balls back in elementary school becomes fields of energy and packets of information. Scientists have studied matter at the coldest levels. The level at which all matter ceases to vibrate is called zero point and what they have found is that even at zero point there is still a field of energy.

Classical physics looks at energy and describes it as something with the capacity to do work. We know that energy exists in many forms and states. We have light energy, nuclear energy, chemical energy, thermal energy, mechanical energy and electrical energy. Those are just the ones that we know and work with every day. I am sure there are many other forms of energy in existence that we haven't seen and worked with as yet. On a Newtonian physics level, energy certainly does work. It moves and flows through everything. It can never be destroyed, but it can be converted into another form and in the process performs work.

For example, when we eat vegetables, we are consuming a plant that has converted light energy from the sun through photosynthesis into the fibers of its being. As we eat, our bodies break down the cells of the vegetables and as a result, absorb the energy that is released. That which is not absorbed is passed out of the system as waste. In essence, we are consuming light energy and are transforming it into other forms of energy that our cells can work with.

And finally, we have Source energy. Whether you are mystic or religious, many of us work from the belief and concept that Source energy flows through all things. Current science certainly cannot prove or disprove this belief. But doesn't it make sense that some original energy has to exist for all the other forms of energy to emerge from? Assuming that this is true then, aren't all other forms of energy just Source energy transformed? This brings us to the concept of consciousness.

Consciousness

Since the beginning of mankind, individuals have tried to understand this elusive concept. Though we certainly understand small parts of it, in actuality we have barely scratched the surface. For my purpose, just as I see Source energy flowing through all things, I also see consciousness existing in all things. Human nature, with its ego, likes to associate consciousness with awareness and the brain as a point of reference. I believe this to be extremely limited.

Plant consciousness has been proven for more than a hundred years. My strength has always been in working with the subtle energies of the Earth and the consciousness that resides within the crystals of the world. To me, they are a crystal friend and not just some inanimate object. And then we also have the animal kingdom. More than ever I am seeing individuals that have opened up their abilities to communicate directly with animals. Just because many have not experienced firsthand these types of connections does not make them any less true. We all have these capabilities if we open up to them. One of the consequences of Separation consciousness within our beings is that we also see ourselves as separate from the outside world. We don't feel our connection to Mother Earth and all the energies that exist because we are still working on healing our own internal disconnections.

All the fear, control and competition in this world are merely byproducts of these separations. By introducing the concept of Separation consciousness and the traits associated with it, I am attempting to give a label to the belief structures and actions that come from being separate from our higher levels of consciousness where unconditional love lives and there is no judgment. Over the millenniums, thousands of enlightened individuals have achieved these states. From these individuals and their examples, we know that all things are connected. We have only the illusion of separation. Energy and consciousness are continuously moving through everything in our reality, and as such there is no one or thing that is ever separate from another.

We have each met people who always know the right thing to say; are calm and pleasant; are always supportive. When a crisis comes, they are unruffled and present with the crisis in order to bring it to resolution. On the other hand, we have equally met people who can stub their toe and think the world is coming to an end. Then, of course, there are all of those residing in between. It is the people who are calm and centered, always offering a loving perspective that is sincere and nurturing, that have come into a space of consciousness. All the great leaders of religion—Jesus, Mohammed, Buddha, Confucius—taught one thing and that is love. When you encounter these people who can keep calm and be a blessing in the storm, you've met those that have come into the center of themselves and are emanating the love that all these religions speak to.

Certainly, love is the most important thing that these individuals taught, but there is more to it than just that. They were present in the moment and had transcended fear and judgment. If you wish to move into the higher states of consciousness—and most of us do—take the time to work in these areas. See how present in the moment you can be every moment of the day by being conscious of your thoughts and present with them. Recognize when you are in fear and judgment and learn to re-center yourself in love. That is what self-mastery and self-realization are all about.

Researchers such as Dr. David Hawkins have even come up with a scale placing different aspects of our life experience on a consciousness scale. As you can see, the scale ranges from 1 to 1000, with Enlightenment residing at the 700-1000 level.

Enlightenment	700-1000	Ultimate Consciousness
Peace	600	Pure Joy
Joy	540	
Love	500	
Reason	400	Flow
Acceptance	350	
Willingness	310	
Neutrality	250	
Courage	200	Just Getting By
Pride	175	
Anger	150	
Desire	125	
Fear	100	
Grief	75	Suffering
Apathy	50	
Guilt	30	
Shame	20	

For more than thirty years, Esther Hicks has worked with the group energy known as Abraham. For those of you that have not taken a look at the volumes of information she has produced, please avail yourself of this wealth of information. I cannot recommend her material highly enough.

One of the core understandings that Abraham has conveyed over the years is that we are vibrational beings living in a vibrational universe. Once again, we are back to the concept of everything being energy. The difference in our experiences is determined by the vibration or frequency that we are expressing. Our thoughts are constantly creating our reality and our emotions give us feedback, guiding us toward where we want to go. Life is supposed to be filled with joy and laughter, lived through your passions. It wasn't meant to be a struggle.

You might notice the similarities between the emotional guidance scale and Dr. Hawkins's consciousness scale. The more we function in the higher emotional states of love and joy, the more we simultaneously operate at higher states of consciousness.

Emotional Guidance Scale

1. Joy/Appreciation/Empowered/Freedom/Love
2. Passion
3. Enthusiasm/Eagerness/Happiness
4. Positive Expectation/Belief
5. Optimism
6. Hopefulness
7. Contentment
8. Boredom
9. Pessimism
10. Frustration/Irritation/Impatience
11. Overwhelmed
12. Disappointment
13. Doubt
14. Worry
15. Blame
16. Discouragement
17. Anger
18. Revenge
19. Hatred/Rage
20. Jealousy
21. Insecurity/Guilt/Unworthiness

A core concept of the Abraham/Hicks material is that our emotions are constantly giving us feedback regarding our alignment with our soul's desires. When we have a desire or a direction that our soul wishes to move toward or achieve, part of us moves there instantaneously. This pure energy aspect of ourselves then begins to beckon the rest. In essence, it is that calling we hear in our hearts saying, "come this way." When we are angry or jealous, we are not in alignment with our true energy. As we move up the scale we are literally getting closer to where our energetic body has already gone. All we are doing is closing the gap.

Here are some of the other thoughts that Abraham has conveyed over the years.

- Individuals are physical extensions of the non-physical.
- People are in their bodies because they chose to be.
- The basis of life is freedom; the purpose of life is joy.
- People are creators; they create with their thoughts.
- Whatever people can imagine totally & completely, by creating a perfect vibrational match, is theirs to be, or do, or have.
- Individuals choose their creations as they choose their thoughts.
- Emotions indicate what people are creating, either consciously or subconsciously.
- The universe adores people; it knows their broadest intentions.
- Individuals should relax into their natural well-being, and know that all is well.
- Life is not meant to be a struggle, but a process of allowing.
- People are creators of "thoughtways" on their unique "paths of joy."
- Actions and money are by-products of focusing on joy.
- Individuals may depart their body without illness or pain.
- People cannot die; their lives are everlasting.

- The nature of the universe is infinite and expanding.

- Any desire born in one can be fulfilled.

- Individuals are not only a part of the universe, but are the very source of it.

All of this leads more fully into understandings of the Law of Attraction and how we create our own individual realities.

The Law of Attraction is the concept that everything you do, say and be (your state of being) is constantly interacting with the universe and drawing back to you a similar vibration. This action works 24/7 whether you are conscious of it or not. Every thought, belief and emotion you have comes into play in a constant dynamic dance, creating your reality.

Understanding that we are creators and we are constantly sending information into the universe around us is one of the most important understandings I can pass on to you. You are connected to all that is. If you can begin to work from that point of view, then you will be much more accepting and understanding of how you can help yourself, as well as those around you.

Fields of Energy

We have a physical body, of course. We see it, touch it, and carry it around with us all day long. What most people do not see are the subtle energy fields that exist with it. When we shuffle our feet across the carpet in the wintertime we create static electricity. Then, if we touch something, we see a spark connecting our field with the field that we are touching. When an electrician places an ohmmeter in an electrical socket, he is testing the connection in the field running through the wires. We can touch the prongs ourselves and register on the meter as well. Scientists have used Kirlian photography for a hundred years to photograph the fields of energy around everything we can imagine. We have had a great deal of experience at working with electrical and magnetic fields in our environment. But there are other fields we have not worked with to the same extent and these are the informational fields.

Individuals such as Jesus and other healers have worked with these fields for thousands of years. Unfortunately, traditional medicine based on pharmaceuticals does not. Informational fields carry enormous levels of data and when we work with them we can effect great change in our bodies. These fields act like a hologram providing a blueprint that our bodies align to. When someone has an instantaneous healing you can almost always be assured that something big has changed within their field. When the information inside our field becomes disturbed or corrupted, disease occurs. When coherent information is in our field, we have health. For thousands of years, energy workers have through various means shifted or changed the information in a person's field into a more coherent state, and the body has moved to match it. Scientists actually have a name for these fields. They call them "morphogenetic fields."

The allopathic medical community works on a business model based on expensive surgeries and pharmaceuticals. Instead of embracing understandings about the subtle energy fields and teaching them alongside its other courses of study, traditional medicine has chosen to either ignore or block them. As a consequence, the medical community has clung to a model of healing that is unsupportive of the new children. Hence, I have included a chapter on the subject to hopefully give you a background in this area.

The Unlimited Nature of a Soul and Reincarnation

One of the most important points that I wish to convey is that the children coming on to this planet are highly advanced souls, not just children. When we see them as children, frequently we see them as less than, in need of training. Of course, children need to be cared for, nurtured and loved but they are not a blank slate when they come into this world. Every one of them has a purpose and there is energy within each guiding them toward that end. If we were to see them as the amazing souls they are, I guarantee that we would treat them differently.

One of the main limiting beliefs that those in the west have about life has come from Christianity. It is, that we have only one life. *The truth is that life is a continuum, not a single experience.* I consider the deletion of all the references to reincarnation and past lives from the Bible to be one of Christianity's greatest disservices to its followers.

Buddhism, Hinduism and Islam represent almost half of the world's population and have each kept various forms of understandings of reincarnation and other lives, but Christianity did not. Why this was deleted I truly don't know, but its effect on our understanding and how we treat our children is very evident. Children are thought of as innocent when they are born: blank slates to be filled. We assume that everything they need to know has to be provided by us as parents, taught through school or gained through life experience. We assume that nothing else is brought into their lives.

Part of the reason for this is the veil of amnesia that we go through when our souls move from the spirit side into our physical bodies. Certainly if we remembered all our past lives we wouldn't even be having this discussion. So why do we have this veil? The reason is fairly simple. We learn more as souls by coming in without these memories available to us on a conscious level. That does not mean that we retain no memory. Some of the memories are retained in the cells of the body and some within the subconscious. But normally you will not see them brought to the conscious mind unless they are part of the life path, such as that of a prodigy. Mozart and Tiger Woods both fall into this category. I have no doubt that Tiger had been one of the old golfing masters of Scotland and that Mozart had had a previous life in music. But in general we learn more by not actively retaining our past life memories. In one of my lifetimes, I had been a painter to the king of France. My paintings reside in

19

virtually every major museum around the globe and yet in this lifetime I've never even drawn a sketch.

In my own exploration over the years, I've tapped into lifetimes covering every kind of experience you can imagine. In some lives, I was a very good guy and sometimes not so good. I've been a warrior and a priest, a king and a prostitute, and so on. And those are just the lifetimes on Earth. I have a Master's degree in Mind-Based Medicine. This included extensive study and practice in hypnotherapy and NLP (Neuro-Linguistic Programming). I also studied extensively with Dolores Cannon, who was an absolute master at deep trance hypnosis. Dolores's work is fascinating. What she found was that under deep hypnosis an individual could access his or her higher levels of consciousness that know everything about them. Why they are experiencing a particular pattern in their lives. How they created a particular disease or illness and what they were to learn from it. Why an injury occurred and what their life's purpose was. Why they are here. The list goes on and on. She also found out that instantaneous healings could occur when you were working with this level of consciousness.

Dolores and her daughter Julia compiled the many volumes of information gathered over her more than forty years of work into numerous books. If you are open to expanding your understandings of the universe and life take a look at her material. (http://www.dolorescannon.com/) She has a lot of excellent information that you would benefit from. At the same time, Dolores's information is only one source. There have been numerous other individuals over the last fifty years who have also been given extraordinary understandings of how life and the universe work. The reason this information is coming in now is a simple one: We are ready for it.

Our normal existence as a soul is primarily non-physical. We choose physical existences to broaden our awareness and consciousness. Within our human experiences, we give ourselves the opportunity to experience life in every possible way. Male, female,

20

tall, short, rich, poor, healthy, unhealthy. And these are just the human experiences. You are an unlimited soul; as such you can choose an experience in any form if you wish. You could be a tree or a shrub. You could be a stone or a crystal. You could be another animal type if you wished. On a grander scale, you could be a planet or a sun. When you think of the physical universe as a giant playground with an infinite number of experiences available to you as a soul, then you begin to truly expand your awareness.

In general, if you were to look at an individual's full array of lifetimes, most of them would be fairly common. Dolores called them "meat and potato" lifetimes. As I have traveled around the world, I have had the pleasure of connecting with the energies of many different areas. Sometimes just being there will trigger an old memory or feeling. I found this especially to be true if there was something unhealed from a previous lifetime there. Because I was open and aware during my travels, I benefited greatly from this practice.

Here's a list of some of the more notable ones that have arisen for me to look at over the years. About half of these came up in my travels and the other half came to me out of curiosity as I explored my own past.

> - A member of the house of David
> - Female healer as an Essene
> - Blacksmith in ancient Rome
> - Legion commander in Rome
> - Priest in Egypt
> - Prostitute in Egypt
> - Buddhist monk in Japan
> - Young woman in India
> - Diplomat in Tibet
> - Relative to Genghis Khan
> - Mayan priestess
> - Monk in the Dark Ages
> - Knight in feudal England

- ➢ King in ancient Cyprus
- ➢ Farm boy in the old West
- ➢ Male child in Mexico
- ➢ In World War II, my soul had two lifetimes going on simultaneously. I was a pilot on the German side and a foot soldier on the American.
- ➢ In Atlantis, I was a crystal gardener. I grew the giant crystals.
- ➢ Many different lifetimes in Hawaii
  - ○ A female priestess
  - ○ A warrior
  - ○ A nobleman and chief

Still, the main reason for mentioning all of this is for you to have a better understanding as to where I'm coming from when I look at a child. A child is a soul that has had a continuum of lifetimes. Some on Earth and perhaps some elsewhere, since the soul is unlimited in its choices.

Points to Remember

1. We are at the end of a great cycle.

2. The paradigms and structures of fear, judgment and competition do not serve the new children.

3. For a parent or grandparent, it is important to remember we are constantly modeling for our children.

4. These children are like a brand-new computer and the programs of the past are not in alignment with their consciousness.

5. The conditioning of our children goes all the way back to the point of conception.

6. Everything is energy.

7. We are vibrational creatures living in a vibrational universe.

8. We are far more than just our physical body.

9. Life is not a single lifetime, it is a continuum, and as an unlimited soul we can choose from an infinite number of choices the experiences that we wish to have.

2

Mankind is Constantly Evolving

Mankind is constantly evolving, but over the last seventy years the level of change has occurred exponentially. In this chapter, I share with you many of the things going on behind the scenes causing this acceleration and what the Quantum children have to do with it. Just who are the Quantum children anyway?

Mankind is constantly evolving. But when you take a step back and look at all that has occurred since World War II, it is easy to see that the pace of our evolution has quickened enormously. So, perhaps a little understanding of what is going on globally for the Earth as well as humanity would be beneficial.

For thousands of years, humankind has been operating within a level of consciousness that is known as third density. The term **density** is used because it is a specific vibratory rate and level of consciousness. Sometimes you will hear references to third, fourth and even fifth-**dimensional** space, and this can get confusing for some because they already have an association in their minds about what a dimension is. They are naturally thinking about height, width and depth, and the physical universe that we are in. Because I am talking about levels of consciousness, I will normally use the term *density* instead of *dimension* just for clarity. When we think of density we might also think of something as being either light or heavy. As an example, love has a very high vibration and is very light in its density. At the other end of the scale, you have fear, anger and hate, which have a very low vibration and are very dense.

When we think of human nature on Earth, our minds are naturally describing life in third density because this has been our point of reference for such a long period of time. This is what we know.

We can think of all the good in the world and all the evil. We can see images of love and we can see pain; however, more than anything else, it is competition, control and fear that dominate this level of awareness. This is why third density can be so destructive. I enjoy referring to third density as Separation consciousness because we are acting as if we are separate from one another. All forms of domination or discrimination, obviously, are part of this limited awareness; however, this separation isn't real. It is an illusion and when we break out of it, all forms of shifts in consciousness can occur.

Eons ago, as a group consciousness, we had set this timeframe as the time that we would have graduated from third density and moved on into the higher vibrations of the fourth. However, after two world wars and the use of the atomic bomb, our energy had stalled and we were woefully behind on where we had wanted to be. Our consciousness was also not at the right level to use nuclear power with peace and integrity. We were like children playing with a loaded pistol and nothing good was going to come of it. Thus, it was determined on the spirit side that something significant had to occur.

There are councils of light that are constantly monitoring our progress as well as that of the Earth's. It is vital to understand that the Earth has her own ascension path just as we humans do, and she was ready to move into her next level. The problem was that we weren't ready. Everything that exists on Mother Earth has to be able to work in harmony with the core vibrations she holds. However, at the time, our energy was not anywhere close to being able to make the shift with her and there was a high likelihood of something cataclysmic happening. This was back in the 1940s.

Two courses of action were chosen by the light councils to avert the impending train wreck. Mother Earth, through her grace, extended us an additional transition period. She delayed her movement into fourth density by almost seventy five years, with her full transition occurring in 2012. It was also determined that if enough souls of a higher level of consciousness volunteered to come and experience life on Earth, our energy could be shifted. We had stalled and something had to be done to get us out of the rut we were in. Thus, a call for help went out throughout the cosmos and billions of souls responded. Yes, I said billions. Of this group, approximately fifty million were selected and are living regular lives on Earth.

Meet the Starseeds

Their job was to bring in such a level of love and light that all of the mass consciousness would begin to shift. Dolores Cannon found in her research three different waves of souls that have volunteered to have lifetimes on Earth since World War II. I believe there were possibly even more.

I really have to laugh sometimes at all the fear-mongering in various movies about aliens and ETs. All of us probably have had lifetimes elsewhere in the universe and could confirm this if you really wanted to look into it. The main difference between one of the volunteers and someone that has had most of their lifetimes here is that the former's consciousness was higher and they weren't tied in to the karmic wheel that so many of us have journeyed through. Even though they might not have karma to work through does not mean that a life here would have been easy for them. On the contrary, it has been very difficult for many of them. This was due primarily to the level of negativity that still existed here.

For thousands of years, we have used reincarnation and karma as our primary ascension tools. Those of us that have experienced many lifetimes here on Earth would use these tools over and over again to experience both love and all that is not love. Ideally, we would have only loving thoughts toward everyone, but of course, this doesn't happen as much as we would like. When we hurt or injure someone physically or emotionally, this energy is going to need to be balanced. In the past, we had the luxury of carrying this energy forward into another lifetime but with our time in third density coming to an end this is no longer the case. Karma in its simplest form can be seen as a balancing of these expressions. It is important also to understand that any karma we take on is imposed by ourselves. No one is doing something to us.

The Starseeds, for the most part, had little or no karma that they needed to balance; consequently, they have fewer balancing experiences to go through. It is much easier for them to hold a space of love and help all humanity do the same. This is how we broke out of the hole we had dug for ourselves.

Others within the Baby Boomers

There was another large group that also came in with the Baby Boomers. It was comprised of individuals who had spent many, many lifetimes here. Many of us have had lifetimes in Ancient Lemuria and Atlantis, not to mention other places and periods. After the fall of Atlantis, many of us worked in the numerous mystery schools around the planet maintaining and keeping the higher levels of wisdom until all of humanity was ready. Egypt housed probably the largest of the mystery schools, along with the Druids in Great Britain, the Yogis in Asia and the Essenes in the Middle East. Many of these individuals had already moved into the next levels of consciousness from their Earthly lifetimes. As such they were very familiar with life here and would be perfect way-showers.

Their energy, combined with that of the early Starseeds, spawned the awakening that later turned into the New Age movement of the 1960s, 70s and 80s. Their awakened, intuitive gifts and greater understanding of the metaphysical world helped open the door for all of us to tap into many of our abilities that have lain dormant within us. All of us have aspects of consciousness that we have just started to reawaken. These two groups have been the way-showers.

Just like the Starseeds, this group of Baby Boomers also carried in very little, if any, karma. They were here to be of service to all humanity.

Magically, after their arrival, the peace movement and the civil rights movement of the 1960s came into being. Feminism began to break down some of the barriers and belief structures women faced. But this was only the beginning. The structures of society also had to be addressed, consequently a new group began arriving in the late 60s.

Indigo Children

The predominance of the Indigo children arrived in the 80s and 90s. Some estimates indicate that more than ninty percent of the children born in the mid-90s were Indigos.

Societies build structures that are in alignment with their consciousness. These structures not only mark our paths through life but also provide something that we tether our identities to. They provide stability and constancy, and are very resistant to change, especially if there is a large degree of power housed there. Whereas initially these structures may have been beneficial, when it is time for a change the opposite becomes true. Structures by nature are static and filled with the consciousness under which they were formed. Consequently, when a society is ready to shift and move forward, a structure becomes a ball and chain to those that have their energy tied to it. Look at the public school system. It was designed to create factory workers at the turn of the century. Everything about it is aligned with being compliant to authority and adhering to rigid rules. The new children need so much more.

Structures can be changed from within or they can be bypassed by a new structure. On the one hand, changing a structure from within would be ideal, but frequently this isn't the case. The individuals involved do not wish to lose or relinquish any level of power. They feel threatened and will do anything and everything to maintain the status quo. On the other hand, bypassing the old structure by building a new one that makes the old one obsolete normally is an easier way.

Enter the Indigo children. These are our structure-busters and structure-builders. These children were discovered initially by Nancy Ann Tappe in her research into the life colors she was seeing in people's auric fields in the early 70s. This color fell on the spectrum between blue and violet and it was one she hadn't seen before. There is a great deal of excellent material written about the Indigos if you would like to know more. For our purpose at present, let me give you just a thumbnail sketch.

The Indigo children are known for their warrior spirit and work to dissolve any structure that lacks integrity. They are intolerant of absolute authority, rituals and institutions that do not function ethically or are cumbersome, such as legal systems, government, big businesses and activities. Indigo children can sense dishonesty like a dog can sense fear. And since their collective purpose is to usher us into a new world of integrity, the Indigo's inner lie detectors are integral.

A classic example of an older Indigo would be the filmmaker Michael Moore. Michael is best known for his documentaries. In 1997, his movie *The Big One* spoke about the mass layoffs in America during a time when the corporations were having record profits. These companies were outsourcing to cheaper labor pools in Asia. In 2002, Michael's movie *Bowling for Columbine* won the Academy Award for best documentary. It probed the culture of guns and violence in America. In 2005, *Fahrenheit 9/11* was nominated for even a higher award: that of the Academy's Best Picture. This movie examined America in the aftermath of 9/11, and the actions of the Bush administrations and their connections with Osama Bin Laden. *Sicko* looked at a broken health industry and *Capitalism, a Love Story* viewed the rape of America by the big financial houses of Wall Street during the financial crisis of 2007-2010. Moore's latest, *Where to Invade Next*, is my favorite of all of them.

The Indigos were born into this world at a higher frequency than the generation before them. Many of them also came in with their intuitive and psychic gifts already awakened. As each of us moves into higher frequencies, our own latent gifts in these areas will begin

29

showing themselves as well. For example, telepathy is one ability that is within every one of us and it is manifesting more and more in the new children coming in.

All the new groups of children are extremely sensitive. In order to work at the higher frequencies, you have to be — and this has been one of their biggest challenges. The Indigos are both emotionally and environmentally sensitive and this manifests in sensitivity to foods, dyes, world events, and peoples' moods. You can imagine how difficult it might be for them in school with the level of stress they could be subjected to. Within the medical community, standard practice and dosages were set up for my generation. Because of their sensitivities, the dosages used by the medical community naturally were going to be too high. Being the type of structure that the medical community is, it has been very slow to adjust and this has consequences.

In general, the Indigos are right-brain dominant in their thinking, which enhances their creativity. This right-brain dominance, however, clashes with the repetitive learning common in education and has caused many of them to be diagnosed with ADHD or ADD. This is a perfect example of a structure not adjusting. Instead of seeing itself as the problem, it deems that the problem lies with the child and hence prescribes medication to control them. Needless to say, we will talk more about the structure of education in Book two because it is one of the most important that we deal with on a daily basis.

As I delved deeper into my understandings of the different groups, it was explained to me in a channeling with Lesley Michaels that souls are coming onto our planet in groups that are far more varied in size than we normally are aware of. Commonly we look at generations in a linear fashion, with a period of twenty-thirty years being standard. The Baby Boomer generation, as an example, is looked at as all those individuals born between 1946 and 1964. Then we had what was coined as Generation X, which referred to those born between 1965 and 1984, and then we had the Millennials. What actually is occurring are groups come in over a much shorter period of years. Seven years is the most common size group and instead of entering in a linear sequence, the groups overlap. I mention this to you as just something to be aware of and not to try to come up with a new set of labels.

This seven year style has been ongoing for a very long period of time, but because the differences within the groups were very subtle in previous generations they weren't noticed. As a consequence of the accelerated progression of those already on the planet and those who will be entering, there is greater differentiation between the new children of this generation and the new children of the previous wave of seven years. Within each wave there will be those who are rare: the first-comers. Then there will be a great body of those children coming in, followed by a gradual slowing as the next generation of seven years starts its preparations and selection of when, where and how it will be entering the planet.

Within each group of early-comers are those who are able to break through great paradigms of ideas and beliefs, and in doing so begin laying an energetic foundation for others to follow. Once the paradigms have been broken, the bulk of the group is able to move the entire experience to a new level. Einstein was an early-comer of his group. Martin Luther King, Jr. was early in his as well, with his prominence coinciding with the peak recognition of that entire generation of seven. Go back to the time of the great sea voyagers and the common understanding that the Earth was flat. Early ones such as Galileo are still spoken of. This pattern that we are working with is an old one, and as such there's no need to fear the level of change that the new children are bringing in. They will be breaking through a lot of old beliefs and ideas, and this is a great gift to all of us.

Crystal and Rainbow Children

Several other groups of children have begun to be identified. In the mid-90s, children with an opalescent color in their auric field began showing up and were named the Crystal children. Much like the Indigos, these new children are extremely sensitive, but as they blend their energy with the Indigos, their job is quite different. A

31

crystal, for example, helps to bring clarity and focus to anyone using it. It also helps to blend and harmonize. Just like its namesake, that is very much what these children do. In many ways, the new children are the perfect foil for the Indigos. They work very well in groups and will help harmonize the myriad changes that must take place as we move away from Separation consciousness.

The Rainbow children began showing up in the 2000s. Not surprisingly, their name was coined by the colorings that were seen in their field as well. They are a delight. Their joy, their love, adds a softness to everything they touch. They soften, blend and merge the overall effect of the enormous changes occurring within the human grid. In many ways, they are the glue that will hold the fabric of reality together when all the stresses of fear try to tear it apart. They are magical on so many levels. These children are an absolute joy to be around. They are like love personified, not that the other children aren't love as well, but I think you know what I mean.

Since September of last year, I've been working with Anna Lys in my meditations. She is an early-comer in another set of souls that are ready to come in as well. So, as you can see, it doesn't stop. Group after group are coming in to help with the shift, so to simplify things I'm going to refer to all of them as the "Quantum children." The term quantum refers to the concept that these children are aligned for Unity consciousness, not separation. It is through quantum physics that we have begun to understand at a much greater level how all things are connected. These children also represent a quantum leap in consciousness. Their mind, body and soul are aligned for the new world that is being created, not the old.

These Quantum children are providing us with an example of where we are moving to, and we have a great opportunity to model them as we move through our own shifts.

All the new children are plugged into the higher dimensional planes. Where the Indigos had some difficulty with focus, the new children don't have the same difficulty. Still, structures of society are very quick to label and many children are said to be ADD or ADHD when they are not. This is a very common behavior of the medical community and the big pharmaceutical companies. It seems they have to create a problem in order to sell their products. You as a parent have to be strong to resist the pressures that these structures will bring to bear against you. The Quantum children are as they were meant to be. That does not mean that you feed them sugar and think it will be okay. Because of their sensitivities, their diet is extremely important.

In order to break through the old ideas and paradigms, the Indigos had to have a warrior spirit, which challenged and threatened the Establishment. The new children since then are gentler in their temperament. The thing I'm normally most impressed with is their awareness. It is off the charts. Many of them act far older than their years. These are old souls that are coming in and they are amazing.

Each of us is part of a group of souls with a purpose. Whether you have been given a special name or not does not matter. If you are here, you are here for a reason. As for myself, I am an Earthkeeper. For hundreds of thousands of years, I've had lifetimes working with Mother Earth in various capacities. The most unique characteristic I have is a fiber of Mother's energy grid within my own. In many ways, it's not unlike your connection with your own children. Much of my understanding is related to this connection because I feel Mother at levels that few people on the planet can. Our group is small. We number only about three thousand and yet I've had no problem meeting and connecting with others over the years. When I'm with another keeper I just feel it. You can't explain it because it doesn't come from the mind. It comes from the knowingness inside of you.

Each of the Quantum children has talents, gifts and uniqueness that they wish to express. Love them fully with all your heart and celebrate their uniqueness. In the past, society stressed doing anything and everything to fit in, to be normal. Well, normal is relative and your image of normal probably is not the same as a previous groups' and why should it be? Will you celebrate their uniqueness or will you fight to suppress it? We are in a time of great change and those of us that are flexible, creative and adaptable will flourish. Embracing our individual uniqueness is an important part of our moving forward with new perspectives and beliefs on life.

With every new group of children, our mass consciousness is ratcheted another notch higher, so more of our authentic self is being revealed. Live from your greatest version of your authentic self and see where that takes you. I'm sure you will be amazed.

Each Group has a Purpose

When we talk about children what we are really talking about are souls. Souls that have evolved to a certain level and are coming into a physical experience as humans on planet Earth. The goal of every parent and the education system should be to help each individual uncover their gifts and find ways for them to be expressed to aid all of society. Sadly, this is not the case.

Every one of us has genius within. Not some of us. Not most of us. Every one of us. We just have to keep exploring until we find it. Some of us find and connect with our passions early in life while others may not discover them until much later. Sir Ken Robinson has been writing and speaking for decades on the subject of finding one's Element—that magical combination where passion meets talent. If you have not looked at his understandings before now, please take the time to do so.

Normally, we look at genius in a classical sense, but what if our genius doesn't lie within our intellect or some other trait that we could perhaps make a career out of? What if our genius is in the ability to express love unconditionally or the gift of being compassionate even under the most trying of circumstances? Would you still see it as genius and honor it in the same way?

Prior to an incarnation one's soul draws up and creates a very elaborate life chart. Placed within it is everything you could imagine that pertains to your life. Your passions and gifts, of course, are part of this chart. But an interesting challenge occurs as we move from the non-physical realms through the birthing process. We pass through a veil that gives us amnesia. We forget everything. To counter this, a great deal of what we desire to experience is coded within us at the silicon level of the cells. Some of it is available to us immediately, but the rest is time-coded for later periods of life when it is appropriate. We also have our guides and angels constantly talking to us in dream states. So regardless of how we access the information, the fact is that we have a lot coming to us and within us. The question is, "Are we listening?"

One of my favorite analogies is that life is like a play. We are the playwright, the lead actor, the director and the producer. And within the concept of Free Will Choice, we have full improvisational capability within any scene of the play. We have gone to very great deal of time and trouble to hire a whole cast of characters (friends and family) to play all sorts of various roles for us, and we will spend an entire lifetime playing through the numerous acts of our play. In order to help us remember at least some of our lines, we encode the script into time-released strips within our cells. It is like having our own personal cheat sheet within each of us. The key to untapping this information is within each of our abilities to live from our heart, because it is through our heart that we receive our soul's information, not the brain. Unfortunately, a great deal of society has been conditioned to stay so much within their minds that their brain chatter won't let anything else be heard. Daily meditation is one of the simplest methods anyone can use to begin to quiet all the noise and really begin to tap into all that is available to you.

We also have the benefit of our guides and our angels that have full access to all our information. Think of them as assistants standing in the wings of the stage with cue cards, giving us information about which direction to go. All we have to do is listen.

Unfortunately, many people are so "closed down" it would take a loudspeaker to get the messages through to them. A quiet mind is such an important thing to have in today's world. Certainly, as a parent, it would be extremely beneficial to reawaken your own capabilities in this area and pass them on to your children.

One of the most intriguing groups that we work with over the millenniums is our soul family. This is a much smaller group of individuals that are close to us in many regards. For example, they are normally at a very similar evolutionary level. I've never heard a reason for the exact size of an individual's group. However, it has been my experience to find that the groups normally number anywhere from fifty up to several hundred. Without a doubt, though, they are probably the most important group that we draw from when we are looking for cast members for our play. Most of you would be surprised at the myriad of roles you have played for one another. One time you might have been the mother and another time the son. Every combination is possible. When you look at those you have chosen to be close to you and see them acting a certain way toward you, consider that perhaps they are doing nothing more than playing the role you asked them to play.

In one example, a woman chose one of her closest friends as a soul to be her mother-in-law. We know that mother-in-law relationships can be difficult at best, but this particular woman seemed to go out of her way to push her buttons every opportunity she could get. It was a very difficult relationship, to say the least. But under hypnosis, she was able to see the scene where she was asking this woman (her best friend on the spirit side) to help her with a very specific life lesson. What she had wanted to learn was *tolerance*. Recognizing that her friend was simply playing a role changed her entire perspective and relationship with this other woman.

****

A lot of our happiness is tied to how closely we are living the path that we set for ourselves prior to jumping into this world. One's individual path is paramount, but there is also group energy and purpose coming into play. For the Quantum children, that purpose is a simple one. It is...

To teach humanity to stop <u>DOING</u> life
and to start <u>LIVING</u> life

To find the joy, to find the happiness,
and to live it with great enthusiasm.

To put anything more upon a child
than that will stymie them.

Since these children are coming in for the purpose of spreading joy, it **requires being present in the moment**. Help them experience art, dance, sports or any other activity that requires focus. It will serve them exceptionally well.

My generation had an entirely different focus. And this was to bring in the initial awakening. Our job was to bring awareness to the fact that there is something more than just the physical life. That life was more than just being born, slaving through it and then dying. There is more, much more.

There is a spiritual realm and you are a part of that realm. You are Spirit **living** in a physicalized form. **Living** being the key because there was not much living going on before my generation. It was primarily focused on **doing**. Now, there are still a lot of doers on Earth and we have plenty of room for improvement, but it has gotten better. It is just that we still have a long way to go.

Points to Remember

1. Mankind is constantly evolving.

2. The term **density** is used because it is a specific vibratory rate and level of consciousness.

3. These Quantum children are providing us with an example of where we are moving to and we have a great opportunity to model them as we move through our own shifts.

4. Each group has its own purpose.

5. The purpose of the Quantum children is to teach humanity to stop Doing life and to start Living life.

6. Help the new children find joy and happiness and live it with great enthusiasm.

7. The Quantum children are aligned with Unity consciousness. Belief structures based in Separation will act like a computer virus within them.

3

Zack's Story

Now I want you to meet Zack. Little Zack was born on October 26, 2000, at 6:33 pm in Denver, Colorado. He was a super preemie and weighed only one pound and five ounces, and this is his story. I've known Zack's parents, Anne and Tom, for a long time now. They are a wonderful example of the challenges and successes that await families that are gifted with one of the Quantum children. This story is as much about Anne and Tom as it is about Zack. Put yourself in their shoes as you read this chapter and think how you might have handled some of their challenges.

Zack was greatly desired. Anne and Tom had always wanted children and they already had a daughter, Jessica, from a previous marriage. Tom and Anne had been together for about five years when they decided that the timing for another child was finally right. They did not want to force it and were content to just wait and see what happened. It was two and a half years later when Zack was born. At the time, Anne was thirty seven years old and Tom forty six.

Anne had a genetic ultrasound at about twenty weeks and everything was perfect. The baby was growing well. Anne was happy and healthy. She and Tom came away from the check-up feeling wonderful, knowing that they were going to have a little boy.

Prior to the pregnancy, they had had fun picking out names. Zack was one of the main contenders,so it was fun to start talking to him and calling him Zack even though they hadn't decided on a final name. As Anne would walk the dog, she would have fun singing and talking to Zack. Life was blissful and the excitement was building. It was three weeks and two days later that Master Zack decided he was

39

going to come early and Anne began having contractions. Anne checked into the hospital and the initial exam found that she was already dilating. The doctors felt that they could stave off the contractions with medication and keep the pregnancy going, especially since Anne had been so healthy.

As I mentioned earlier, on a soul level, it is the child that determines the circumstances of his or her birth. Our normal existence is that of spirit. Thus, the choice to have a physical experience, and all that goes with it is never taken lightly and requires extensive planning. As divine souls, we choose all of our individual components of this experience. One of the most important choices we make is certainly our parents' and all the potentialities that a lifetime with them would provide. As souls, we are co-creating long before we ever enter the womb. We do not become creators at a later time in life. We simply ARE.

When the doctors found out that Zack was coming rapidly, they attempted to hold off the delivery for a couple more days. At twenty weeks and two days, Zack was born far earlier than anyone believed to be healthy or possible. Most children born between twenty three and twenty four weeks just don't make it and frequently, those that do have extensive complications. Therefore, you can imagine the mindset of the staff, both nurses and doctors. To them, the outcome was already predetermined. Anne was surrounded by people that were certain this baby wouldn't live, or that if he did he wouldn't live long. If finally, by some miracle Zack managed to survive, he would live a horrible existence attached to a bunch of machines for the rest of his life.

We live life only in the present moment. We create in the present moment. All the projections, all the fears that the doctors and staff had at the hospital are a perfect example of the consciousness that we are moving out of. It pulls us out of the NOW. We create by focusing, and what we focus on is in a constant state of expansion. Anne knew this.

Finally, that night with the company of a beautiful young nurse, Anne was able to get some quiet time. As Anne separated herself from the chaos of the day, she thought to herself, "This is nuts. Not that long ago we were in the land of happy. This just doesn't make any sense." Anne watched the heart monitor and calmly went within to talk with Zack.

"Hey, what's up? What are you doing? What is all this about? Are you okay?

With crystal-clear clarity Zack responded, "Yep. I'm fine. Don't worry. I'm just fine."

The voice had come through her so pure and felt so good that she knew staying connected with Zack and not buying into the doctors' fears was the only way to proceed. None of the chaos that had earlier surrounded her that day matched the way she felt about Zack in her life and about life as a whole.

Anne told Zack she would do her best not to pay too much attention to all the craziness and to just ask him from now on what he needed or wanted; he would have to promise to find a way to tell her. At the time, even though she had gotten such a nice clear response, Anne had her own doubts whether she would be able to know the signs or hear the signals from Zack if things got too chaotic. With Zack's promise, an invisible handshake formed that evening between Anne and her unborn son. She was finally able to fully relax and get some sleep to prepare for the craziness of the next day.

As the day unfolded, the time came to deliver her little boy. Anne realized she was uncertain about what she was supposed to do. She hadn't taken a Lamaze class yet and she wasn't sure when she was to push or how the delivery was to proceed. Anne's doctor was reconciled to the fact that this baby was a goner. She had tried to console Anne, telling her that it was okay and that she could try again later.

It was only a little while into the delivery that the contractions stopped. Everything became still and Anne instinctively knew this wasn't very good. It was at that time that she got a message from Zack. "Hey, you've got to do something. I'm just sitting in here and this isn't doing me any good." Therefore, Anne looked up at the doctor and said, "May I push?" The doctor's response was, "It really doesn't matter. Do whatever you want." Anne dismissed the depressed tone from the doctor and said, "Fine, here we go. Come on." Anne pushed and out came little Zack, all one pound and five ounces of him.

Prior to the delivery, a specialist in premature birth had come into Anne's room and wanted to know if they should do all that they could to save his life using everything they had available. Anne told her that Zack will tell you if he was ready. You will know when he comes out if he wants all the equipment or not. It's not my choice. He will be viable and want to live or he won't. It will be very clear and you guys better pay attention because you are not going to be able to consult with me. You are probably going to show me the baby briefly and then whisk him off somewhere. If you are paying attention, you will know if he's chosen to stay and hang out with us or not. The doctor was very startled, but said, "Okay." Sure enough, little Zack came out flailing and ready to go. There was no doubt that he was here to stay.

He scored eight out of ten on the Apgar scale, which measures a newborn's viability. The doctors look at a child's coloring, breathing and reactions. In Zack's case, he was doing wonderfully, but his lungs were weak and he could only manage a squeak. He just didn't have enough power in his young lungs to make noise. The mood of the doctors and the nurses perked up immediately. They knew they had a fighter on their hands.

Their first challenge was to get Zack stabilized. Even their smallest incubating tube would barely fit in his throat and he was moving so much that he knocked it out three times. Finally, they succeeded, but by then little Zack was exhausted. He had given it all he had and physically it was rough going for the little guy, but his spirit remained very strong. Tom and a couple of their friends were in the

42

room shortly after the delivery. Instinctively, Anne asked if it would be okay for them to sing happy birthday. So it was that young Zack was greeted with a song and a celebration upon his arrival.

Zack was taken to the special neonatal unit at Children's Hospital and Anne stayed that night at Lutheran Hospital. She felt strongly connected to him, and every chance she got she reached out and spoke to him with her thoughts.

Life was an odyssey for the next four and a half months with Zack at Children's Hospital. Anne and Tom visited him virtually every day. The only request the hospital had made was that if they had a cold or were not feeling well, they wait until they got better before coming, but that was infrequent. Anne and Tom also knew that Zack was very capable of using his resources. Anne and Tom agreed that they weren't going to ruin their lives in the process of Zack getting well. They had a household to run; a daughter, Jess, who also needed attention; a dog; and finally, they had each other to pay attention to as well. They were determined to have a beautiful, healthy, happy home for Zack to come home to.

There were some people that were concerned that Anne and Tom were not with Zack 24/7, but this is very much a projection of their own fears and judgments. It was very helpful when Anne and Tom finally were able to have greater input in to the nursing staff and other individuals that were taking care of Zack. This occurred in the third month. They were looking for people that were very positive and most importantly, unafraid of whatever condition that little Zack was going through at the time.

Frequently, Anne and Tom would be asked to make long-term decisions about his care, and consistently they would reply, "Why don't we just go with today." Anne did a wonderful job of staying in the moment, always visualizing him healthy and strong. One day, years later, when Zack was ten years old, Anne turned to Tom and said she had just seen the boy she had been visualizing all those many years ago in the hospital. Zack had been running outside with the dogs. He was the exact image that she remembered with clarity that she had experienced in the hospital. It was such a beautiful moment.

Anne had an interesting contrast of people she came in contact with in the hospital. In general, they either thought she was extremely special or nuts. Why? Because of how happy she was. At three different times, Anne was offered medication by doctors who felt she must be suppressing something. They were projecting that she should be dismal and depressed instead of happy. In many ways, Anne was a beautiful teacher for them. We all teach more through our actions and how we live life than we ever do with our words. Anne would be so excited when she went to visit Zack. The hallway at the hospital would light up in front of her and it would seem like she was practically floating. To Anne, it was like she was following this trail of beautiful light toward him.

Anne and Tom are so grateful for all the inspired caregivers at Children's Hospital. Little Zack got the best of everything. They had been at the hospital for only a few days when a beautiful nurse practitioner who was doing graduate work approached them with an offer. She was looking for children and parents to participate in a new way of caring for premature babies. She wanted to make their environment friendlier, less noisy, less intrusive and less chaotic. She was just the most wonderful woman. Anne still remembers, ten years later, her asking if they would like to participate. Anne responded, "Well, you are asking us if we would like to ride in a Pinto or a Cadillac. I think I'll take the Cadillac. Thank you. It's quite alright for you to swaddle my baby daily and to give him breastmilk on a cotton ball so that when he gets fed through the feeding tube, he experiences the sensation of smell along with getting fed." Another important aspect of Zack's care was that the times people could give him care were carefully planned so Zack could have consistent time during the day when he had peace and quiet, and was not constantly hassled or poked.

Tom and Anne quickly found a routine to keep them in touch with their son. They would call the unit where Zack was cared for each morning between five thirty and six thirty to catch the night nurses before they went off their shift at seven a.m. Anne would be at the hospital during the day, and Tom would visit after work in the evening. They knew it was important that they continue to treat Zack like he was still in the womb, so they would talk or sing to him in soft voices and gently touch his foot or hand. Anne would sing lullabies and Tom would read *The Little Engine That Could*. They recorded their voices to play for Zack when they weren't at the hospital. Anne and Tom knew that the best thing for Zack at that time was to sleep and grow. It was an exciting day a couple of weeks later when Anne and Tom were finally able to hold Zack. Everyone knows how important loving touch is to a human and this is especially true with a newborn. In Zack's case, it had taken several weeks before they could get him stable enough to give him what the staff called "kangaroo care." With all the tubes and equipment around, it took many hands to place him on the bare skin of one of his parents' chests. Once there, it seemed like neither party would want to separate. Anne and Tom would hold Zack for hours at a time. It was very special.

One of the interesting aspects of the hospital that Anne and Tom had to deal with was the fact that it was a teaching hospital. Some staff they could pick as their core crew for Zack, but the doctors would change every four weeks. Because it was a teaching hospital, medical students (fellows) would come and go and seemingly at the right time; when someone had run out of ideas, someone else would magically appear who had an alternative that would work. This is manifesting at its best.

Zack's lungs had been slow in developing and repairing themselves, so he had been on a respirator far longer than anyone would have liked. One morning, a doctor came in with a team of students that he was lecturing. This man was the specialist, supposedly the best in his field and yet right in front of Anne, as if she wasn't even there, he told the team that this child, Zack, would never breathe on his own without the assistance of a respirator. Zack had chronic lung deterioration and such cases were incredibly sad. He then walked away with his group of students.

Anne immediately thought to herself, "You don't know this," and she said to Zack, "We're going to **know** that you're okay!" Sure enough, with the next doctor change, a young doctor came into the picture and had an idea of using a different kind of respirator for Zack. The ones they traditionally use force air into the lungs. This is opposite from the way we naturally breathe. The doctors know that after a certain timeframe, respirators start doing more damage than good to the lung tissues. This doctor had the idea to use an oscillating vent, which would literally give puffs of air gently four hundred times a minute to Zack's lungs. Normally, these types of respirators are used only in a crisis situation. This doctor put him on it for a solid week, and lo and behold, his lungs started to get better. Every time Zack needed something that was different from the norm, he magically would get it. Constantly, the right people would show up for the current situation and Zack would inspire them. It was amazing to watch and to be a part of for Anne.

There are several points I want to re-emphasize here. We are all incredible souls existing in a constant state of creation and this includes our now three pound little Zack. We are each a human soul with a free will choice, but frequently some give their power away to others whom they perceive to be in a position of higher wisdom. This is especially true in the medical field. This is how we have been conditioned. Anne could have bought into the first doctor's opinion and kept Zack on a respirator for so long that his lungs would have become irreparable, but that was not the vision of Zack that Anne had. Anne knew throughout her being that Zack was picking the tools for his toolbox that would ensure him a vibrant life. She had also seen him in her vision as healthy and vibrant. Consequently, she didn't know how the respirator problem would be fixed. She just knew that it would.

46

There are many potentialities swirling around us all the time. The doctor in the first instance saw only one reality and he expressed his opinion as an absolute, from his ego. Zack, Anne and Tom could have chosen to believe what this individual said. We can co-create with another individual. We can buy into that individual's belief system, **but** no one can force their reality on another. Please understand I am not talking about the domination or control of one person over another. This is a mundane expression. I am referring to the internal soul- level energies that no one but you has control over.

Anne never had to call down any of the doctors or nurses. There were always swirling opinions around her, and lashing out emotionally was not her way. Anne didn't have any trouble understanding where the staff was coming from. She and Zack were in a different world and they needed to weave and mesh their energies in that world. Being in the flow with the energies around each of us is one of the most important things we can do in any situation. There were plenty of choices that Anne, Tom and Zack had, even in an environment as restrictive as the hospital setting. As an example, Zack's primary care was handled by a core team of nurses, not the doctors. The doctors might set up the care but it was the nurses implementing it. It was their energy surrounding Zack 24/7. Anne and Tom didn't have too much say about who Zack's doctor was at any point in time but they did have a greater input to the nursing staff. It was pretty much up to Zack to inspire his doctors or to simply wait until they were changed every month. There were always some individuals that would project their fears onto Zack's situation. Anne and Tom would downplay or disregard any of their negative remarks and focus on what these individuals did well.

The recognition and understanding that Zack as a soul was constantly co- creating his situation served Anne and Tom greatly from the very beginning. It allowed them to sleep at night during all those weeks Zack was in the hospital. Some friends envisioned Anne setting up a bed next to Zack and sleeping with all those beeping machines. They somehow felt that obsessing and worrying about him would somehow keep him alive. Anne knew instinctively it would not: that preparing a beautiful space for him to come home to and being sane would. Every night as Anne prepared to go to sleep, she would connect with Zack and say, "You know how to ask for what you want. That was our deal from the get-go. You make sure that you get it. I have a promise from the staff at the hospital, the beautiful nurses that watch you night and day, that no news is good news. I am here. I am available if something changes or something switches. They will let me know." Anne never got a call in the middle of the night. Not a single time.

We do not own our children. We just have the privilege of living with them for a while and interacting with them as they grow up. How you view your children is vital to how you raise them. These children are conscious creator beings and they would enjoy your support along their chosen path. Notice I did not say control or even guidance. In the past, we have felt it was our duty to pass on our morals and beliefs to these children and to teach them right from wrong. We wanted to guide them so that they would not make the same mistakes we made. We wanted them to have a better life than we had. Each of these thoughts, noble sounding as they may be, sees the children as being less than the divine souls they are. Allow them to show you the areas in which they would like to have additional understandings. We are in a mass transition into a fourth density reality. These children are here to guide us. Not the other way around. They know their paths and why they are here. See these children as the old souls that they are, reawakening the ancient wisdom that will move all human consciousness into its next level of existence.

Zack came into this world to live his own life, and Anne and Tom trusted him.

Doctors would come around, evaluate and watch Zack. So much of the condition of preemies and their tentative hold on life is still hugely unknown. Most of the staff, doctors and nurses would say there's only so much they could do, and that is why Zack was such an inspiration to them. This was why it was important for Anne and Tom to hold the space for Zack's energy to move people as well as his own life. There are too many people to name that cared for Zack and loved him during that phase of his young life. Suffice it to say that Anne and Tom and their family will always be grateful and hold in their hearts a very special place for the men and women of the neonatal care unit at Children's Hospital that became, for a time, part of their family.

On March fifteen, exactly one month after his due date and one hundred and fourty days after his birth, Zack was ready to go home.

Home at Last

I asked Anne if she had allowed Zack to help her find a pediatrician as they moved into the next phase of his life. For Anne, it came once again as a very quiet voice within. She had to laugh, though. All these kids are so powerful that she found it was virtually impossible to get in his way. He knows exactly why he's here. He knows what it means to have fun. He knows everything about what he wants and he shows it to Anne time and time again. Anne sometimes would struggle with what she thought she should be doing as a parent in regard to Zack, but ultimately he would always win. Two scenarios would play out for her. She would find herself ready to drop in a heap of exhaustion or be smiling at Zack with a full knowingness that everything had worked out his way with the smallest amount of hassle.

When Zack was about five months old he weighed just under seven pounds. Even though Zack was now about the size of a regular newborn, his body and head were disproportionate. He had a big, blown-up face. There were compromises in Zack's early care, and getting him fed was a major one. When the nurses would attempt to feed him, his oxygen levels would drop dramatically. After all the evaluations and opinions had been given without any success, one lovely nurse came up with the simplest of solutions: We are feeding him too fast. Usually, the solutions for Zack were pretty simple, but a formula that Zack's body liked was never really found. The doctors had him on a high-calorie formula, which made his body very uncomfortable. Anne could see this, but this was one of the areas where she wasn't given a choice and it was frustrating. She and Zack were in their world and between the medical insurance and the hospital there were only so many choices that were open to them — and the choice of formula wasn't one of them. On top of the formula, Zack was being fed a lot of iron for what the doctors considered an anemic condition, and this made him even more uncomfortable. Consequently, Zack came home with a spindly body and a blown-up face. Anne and Tom jokingly would call him Alfred Hitchcock.

They were monitored closely after he came home. It was considered support and was based upon concern for Zack, but it did slow down the implementation of some of the changes Anne felt would have been beneficial for Zack. It was a few weeks before she was able to start backing off on the calories they were putting into the formula so that Zack was more comfortable. To this day, Zack has never really considered eating a huge priority. He was difficult to feed; sometimes it would take hours to feed him, and then he would throw it all back up. His body didn't want to assimilate what they were feeding him, so Anne eventually started taking some liberties. Zack is sixteen now and Anne still laughs at the struggle she had to go through to get him to eat.

The question here is, "What do these Quantum children really need? What does Zack need?" This was the line that Anne and Tom were constantly walking. They understood that he didn't need as much as they did, but they were still uncertain as to what would work best for him. When Zack was a little bit older, Anne would watch him go and go until his little body would just hit a wall and he would crash. Would he tell his mother that he was getting hungry? Of course not; it wouldn't even enter his mind. Many of the children remember so vividly how easy it was to move and exist when they were in a non-physical state that convincing them they are in a human body can be tough. This was where a lot of Zack's feeding issues had their roots. Anne was concerned and recognized early on that this young man had a hard time dealing with the fact that he was now this big energy inside a human body, and that that body required more care.

Sleeping was not high on Zack's list of priorities either. He just never liked to nap. He would just go until his body gave out and then would be a mess. Anne was constantly attempting to figure out the fine line between how little or how much of something he needed. She supplemented his diet with **organic** vitamins, nutrients, calcium, minerals and essential fatty acids. It helped a lot. I would also like to point out that there is an enormous difference in the organic products versus most over-the-counter items that are on the market today. She also gave Zack probiotics consistently. The Quantum children are naturally very sensitive, and Zack was no exception. Anne did everything she could to build up his immune system and his digestive system so that if he wanted to have an ice cream cone on occasion or some other food, it wouldn't end up completely throwing his system off. Zack likes being a kid and Anne didn't want to deny him that human experience.

For Anne and Tom, it was always a delicate balance and they wanted the whole world open to him. Not just the world of play, but the world of food, as well as any other areas of life.

Choices

With Zack being an extreme preemie, the medical community kept Anne and Tom under the microscope. Every three to four months he had a checkup at Children's Hospital. By the time Zack was three, he was thriving, and Anne and Tom were pretty tired of trying to convince everyone of this fact. As for vaccines, they allowed a few of the vaccines, but not all. Usually, Anne would muscle test (applied kinesiology[3]) to decide if something they were putting in his body would ultimately be harmful to Zack or not. She was very

---

[3] See appendix 5 for references

focused on his current state of mind and his vibrational strength. Her sense of feeling concerning the vaccines was correct and Zack never had an adverse reaction to any of the vaccines or medications he was given. She has been able to keep Zack clear of all the auxiliary vaccines, including flu shots.

The problem most parents like Anne and Tom have in regard to vaccines is dealing with various school systems. Even though it is completely legal to opt out of vaccines, school systems frequently ignore the law in this area and the ensuing battle can be a hassle. Zack's current doctor is more aware of nutritional supplements and open to a holistic means of care. Anne was hoping to speak with her about the vaccines prior to Zack's next visit. She knows we are in an area of transition in regard to all forms of medical care and there are only so many battles that one can fight at any one time.

Anne understands the power of one's belief in regard to well-being and the methodologies someone might choose. There are people that truly believe they need vaccines and truly believe that they make them well. There are people that believe just as strongly that they are deadly, so Anne and Tom have been very careful about how they have expressed those thoughts. They did not want to impose their fears onto Jessica and Zack. Regardless of how right they feel about anything, even nutrition, Anne does not wish to create a fear. She plays a game with Zack. She asks him, "How would you feel right now if you just had a big burger and fries?" Sometimes he would say he would feel great and sometimes he would say awful, but asking those kinds of questions gives Zack the gentle reminder to tune within. Anne likes to play this game with activities as well and Zack has gotten really good at being aware of how his body feels at any point in time.

Our bodies are constantly speaking to us, but society as a whole does a poor job of listening. Our bodies are constantly reflecting back to us everything that is going on in our lives. Your body hears and responds to every word you say. Always speak positively about yourself. One of the most powerful phrases in the English language is "I am ..." Use it wisely. Choose to be in love with yourself. It is from that love that you'll be able to see the love within another. Learn to love your body fully. Play with every sense you have every day. They are the magic connecting us to the physical world.

Zack is a huge soul in a tiny body. Being back in the body can be frustrating. Every way you can imagine, develop a love for the body with your child. The Quantum children are so sensitive and so attuned that unless something in their environment such as medication is blocking their ability, it should be very natural and easy for them. Play the "how would I feel if..." game with yourself. The mind is amazing at creating its own virtual reality. You can even change this question around a bit and determine if something is true for you or not. Have fun with it, practice and see what information your body has for you. If you would like to learn more, check out some of the references that I have included in Appendix 5.

In Anne's instance, she never got a sense that the vaccinations would be a problem for Zack and consequently she never chose to fight that battle. Anne's strongest sense of where she had to step in on his behalf was when someone wasn't supportive of Zack's life and the way he was leading it. There was one particular nurse who thought Zack was a lost cause from the very beginning. She thought Anne and Tom were crazy for even keeping this boy alive. They would experience hardship after hardship. She was an excellent technical nurse. The one you wanted to have to get the IV in on the first try, on veins that were so small and fragile, but she just could not see Zack as healthy. Anne just knew it was the places that love comes from that made room for everything to happen perfectly for Zack. Anne's sense at the time was that the timing and the energy of the team surrounding Zack were far more important than any technical aspect of his care.

Anne just knew it was the places that love comes from that made room for everything to happen right for Zack, regardless of methodology.

You would think that Zack would have a huge aversion to the medical community and hospitals. On the contrary, he loves everything about them. He loves to go to the doctor. He loves to go for his well checks. He pulls everything off the walls and luckily, he always gets a doctor who is okay with it. He would have all of their instruments out and he would look through them and hit this switch and that switch. It was candy land for him. Anne used to break out in a cold sweat every time they went, afraid he was going to break something.

He loves the dentist; same thing. He just loves everything around him. He gets them and they get him. In the end, everyone winds up laughing. It's like fairyland and it's been like that since day one. He is the boy everybody marvels at and he is the one that makes it fun again.

Anne has learned more and more not to overlay any of her fears onto Zack. We all have our own sets of beliefs based on our personal experiences and we are welcome to them. In so many ways, Zack has given his parents different ways of looking at things. As your focus shifts, the whole experience shifts. Consequently, Anne has been trained by Zack to allow him his path. For most of the new children the old saying, "less is more" applies. As Anne has found out, it is hard to spoil Zack's day. Even when Anne gets passionate about something, whether it is his school work, or what he is eating, or how he is treating his sister, two seconds later Zack would be whistling and life would be wonderful again.

Many parents feel that they are supposed to be a filter for their children as if they will be able to capture all the bad stuff so only the good comes through. On the one hand, the thought carries the belief that your soul could make you a victim. It cannot, and on another aspect, this thought gives the parent some form of justification for any level of interference they would like to impose. Zack and the other children are so much bigger energetically. Anne could tell from the very beginning that Zack had the soul of a giant. This little guy was full-blown male energy from the get-go and still is. Sometimes he acts as if he would rather be Anne's hunter/gatherer mate than her son. He just has an incredible strength around him and how dare you try to tell him what to do and how to live.

When he was ten, you would have thought that he was ready for his own apartment. He was ready to take charge of his world and we were just getting in the way. He is truly strong. He is like a fifty year old male trapped in this tiny body. He has always had that energy about him. He thinks it is ridiculous and horrible that Anne and Tom can sleep together at night and he has to sleep alone. He says, "If you guys can have someone next to you in bed at night, which is so nice, why can't I?" He started asking this question when he was four.

Zack has always been in constant motion. He hated his crib. To him, it was a cage, but Anne and Tom had to keep him in one because he moved around so much and he was still on oxygen. If Zack wasn't moving on his own and you were with him, he would want to be held but not necessarily cuddled. For Zack, it was like, "hold me mom and let's get moving because I have things to see." He would like nothing better than to be strapped into his little snuggly facing the world while he and his mother took the dog out for her walk. Anne would go and go until finally Zack would fall asleep. Sometimes she would even have to suspend him from a chair to trick him into feeling as if she was still holding him just to be able to go to the bathroom. He wanted to be mobile and Mom was his mobility machine.

When Zack started crawling, he was fast. He didn't start walking, he started running. He was a mother's worst nightmare. You had no idea where he was going. You never knew how far he would hurl himself in any moment. He rarely got hurt, but he did have a couple of good wipeouts. It was just the speed of him that was so daunting. He would never just sit by your feet and play. That was not Zack. When Zack was in the hospital, the nurses on the night shift said he slept very little. He was busy, and he would call out if he was bored so they would come and put him in a jiggly seat and talk to him. Anne and Tom made tapes of their voices with stories and songs on them so that if he woke up in the middle of the night they could play them for him. Zack always needed lots of stimulation.

Anne attempted, as best she could, to teach Zack about the inconsistencies of the world we live in. When we exist in the non-physical planes of the universe, we do not deal with time. If you want it, you have it. If you wish to go somewhere, you are there instantaneously. Your thoughts are transferred telepathically with full emotional content and Zack would remember how effortless everything was. You can imagine how frustrating early life is for these children. Every generation throughout the history of man has had this capability to some degree. Most children start losing the connection by the age of five to seven. However, the veils between the dimensional planes are very weak now. Consequently, many of the Quantum children will be able to hold onto the connection with the other side much, much longer. If you as a parent are very open and accepting of this connection, your children will have the capability of keeping the connection open permanently.

Parents can and often do, however, shut their children down out of fear. We have non-physical beings around us all the time in the form of their guides and angels. They are constantly helping us achieve our desired goals during our lifetime. The more that each of us can free up our lines of communication with this unseen world, the better. Have fun with your children and be open to everything they feel and see. Your accessibility can help immensely.

Can you imagine the difficulty Anne had in trying to describe boundaries and limits to a son who remembers how limitless life truly is? Just trying to describe to him that what he could do with his mother was different than what he could do with the sitter, or what was allowed at school was very frustrating for her. It was just one day at a time watching him grow into his world and she did her best to help him understand the various environments he would be operating in. In the past, parents would focus on discipline and boundaries to create the illusion of stability within the home. These understandings have been a wonderful tool to get us to this point in our development, but they are of the past. They carry far too much of the energy of force to be of value at this time.

Adjusting to this Reality

Throughout all of humanity, the energy of telepathy is slowly being reawakened. The cell phone represents a technological simulation of being able to connect with another individual instantaneously. One must be open, transparent and without fear for this ability to begin to manifest. Children like Zack know how easy it is to communicate in this way. Learning how to read and write, which is sluggish and slow in comparison, was a struggle for him and he resisted it. The way Anne approached it was to remind Zack that he has chosen a human experience for many special reasons. They agreed that his form of communication was far more effective, but in order to interact with the population that is dominant here, it would be beneficial for him to learn to read and write.

From the very beginning, Anne had a strong, open connection with Zack. Most mothers do, but when it came to getting Zack to talk clearly, Anne would know exactly what Zack was asking for, but the utterances coming out of his mouth were more like Russian than English. What I am referring to is much more than the standard toddler learning to talk for the first time. Zack was phrasing and expressing things that were completely incomprehensible to everyone, but Anne knew fully what he wanted. Zack was satisfied with his utterances and he did not want to be bothered with learning a "language." To get him to practice, Anne finally convinced him that it was literally a matter of survival. Anne would have to tell him that she knew what he wanted, but he was still going to have to say it to get it. As you can imagine, this was not a process that Anne enjoyed very much.

It was obvious to Anne that Zack wanted to connect with other people. She saw these struggles with language as just another exploration for him. Zack is not the type of individual that will ever be a loner. He is a lover and a performer and he reaches into people's hearts just by looking at them. Regardless, Anne had concerns about his reading.

Education

Years ago, when Zack was six, I asked what Anne was going to do for Zack school wise. She told me that Zack had wanted to go into the public school system. This really surprised me at the time. It was nice to catch up with her in 2010 to find out how it had worked out. I know Zack had a purpose for choosing a public school, but he was also a perpetual motion machine and I just didn't see that blending in well.

It turned out Zack was very good at following the rules when he was in the classroom. He was a joy to be around and people just loved him. He was learning, but there was a lot of pressure on him. The schooling had a lot of structure and it seemed like people were constantly drawing lines and keeping him in little boxes. Frequently, the children were given little rewards and trinkets for behavior that was unnatural to kids his age. Well, he would come home and just explode. He'd get angry, nasty and uncomfortable with himself. Zack would be able to hold it together during the school day and perform the way he was expected to, but he would be an absolute mess, emotionally and physically by the end of the day, which spurred Anne and Tom to make a change in environments. They were very fortunate to have a charter public Montessori school right around the corner from where they lived and so after two years in a traditional public school, Zack joined an environment where he could move and learn at the same time. This particular school blended both a Montessori curriculum with the standard county curriculum. They would study the same material but in a different way.

Montessori schools encourage the individuality of the kids and the way that they learn. The rate of learning and effective methods vary with each child. Each child is different, and the current school that Zack attends does a very nice job at creating an environment with stimulating tools that inspire the children to learn at their own rate and to grow in the direction they are drawn to. The kids are able to excel and move very quickly through a particular area or take a greater length of time to learn a skill if they choose. The only requirement is that each child accomplishes a certain level of competency before they are allowed to move to the next level. There is far less of a grade level structure that a child has to deal with. Consequently, they are able to flow seamlessly where their heart guides them. Those who still feel a need to compete may argue that the children aren't pushed enough, that life is a struggle and schools that don't push the kids do not prepare them for REALITY. The easiest answer to this judgment is, "Whose reality?"

The standard school systems are designed for the masses and they are highly based on structure and control. All of which is breaking down. They were designed to create factory workers at the turn of the century. This kind of schooling conditions an individual to be a robot. To go out in the workforce, show up on time, punch in your time clock and do your days' work. We tap into all the knowledge of the universe when we are fully present in the moment and are in flow with everything around us. We become timeless. Think of the times in your life when you were so involved with something that you completely lost track of all sense of time. Magnify that by ten and you will know what I am talking about.

Anne has really enjoyed watching Zack grow and learn. He has thrived going at his own timing and pace. His school does do some testing with the Jefferson County curriculum, for instance, reading levels and math. Consequently, Zack still gets an occasional taste of the public school structure. Currently, Zack is progressing nicely in math and his verbal skills are improving. He still has issues with syntax and sentence structure, but who doesn't? Zack is curious about language now and Anne does occasionally see a big spike in his vocabulary. Anne sees his brain as extraordinarily complex. It races miles ahead of where his ability to speak can express. She found that asking him to slow down seemed to help him get his thoughts organized. Getting Zack to focus on his breath also helps a lot. Think of telepathy as being the fastest internet connection possible and speaking to an old dial-up connection. To Zack, it is like he has a stopper in his throat and he can't express what he would like to fast enough. Every day Zack gets better at using the human body as a tool for interfacing with others but it can still be a frustration for him.

On a surface level, Zack would be considered a little behind in his reading, which is deceiving. Anne found out that Zack worked better with descriptions that were more complex. He didn't like the simplicity of the standard children's book. In his case, it is hard to find material that a fifty year-old would enjoy in a book written for a ten year-old. When Zack did find a book that he really enjoyed, he said it was like a movie running in his head. It became that vivid for him. The one thing I would recommend for the Quantum children is to begin reading as early as two. It helps them slow down and enjoy being still from a very early age. Don't force it, but I think you will be surprised at how early these amazing kids can start if they choose.

To Anne, it is obvious that Zack is able to learn whatever he would like to focus on. It just isn't a priority for him to learn in the way that the current system might want him to and that is true for many of these kids.

They don't match up with the current structure

Zack enjoys his Montessori school and until he tells his mom he is ready for a change, Anne and Tom plan to keep him enrolled there. This particular school has expanded and runs through middle school now. Anne volunteers there from time to time and loves being around all the amazing and gifted kids. It also gives her a chance to look at how the children are reacting to the different methodologies of parenting. Some parents attempt to control their children with medication, through discipline, or like Anne—simply carrying on through the day. One of Zack's friends is about to be put on Ritalin and Anne knows it can be a huge life-altering event. Ritalin is an amphetamine frequently prescribed for children considered to have Attention Deficit Disorder.

Society loves to categorize and label. Look at the words: *Attention deficit disorder*. Can you see the judgment your mind immediately goes into when you use this term to describe a child? Can you see the illusion of a child being seen as "less than" when these words are used? The problem is not with the child but with the current society. These children's minds process at levels we can't even imagine. Their neuro-net is wired differently. Their DNA is more advanced. We must move forward to them, but also help them cope and blend their energies with the energies of today.

Now, some children have improved with Ritalin. Some have had little or no improvement and others have died from its usage. Please READ and READ some more about the choices that you as a parent have in this area. Really feel how any particular choice will affect your child, and as I mentioned earlier..."Watch the Dosage!!!!!!" There are options currently available to parents today that did not exist twenty years ago, and they don't involve the use of medications. Please do your research.

Anne is hopeful that the other child's mother is watchful enough and strong enough to take her daughter off the program if any adverse effects show up. She and Tom have been very happy with their choice not to use any medications on Zack, regardless of the fact that taming this perpetual motion machine might ease some of the logistics in their lives.

One of the funny things that Anne and Tom have had to deal with is how Zack looks at time. When you are working in the non-physical planes you are in realms that are outside of space and time. Zack could not care less about time. He does not fuss over it or worry about it. It is just irrelevant. Considering how important it is to be present in any moment, that is not a bad way to be, but for Anne to get him ready for the bus that is coming in five minutes, it poses a challenge. Getting Zack to understand schedules and time was close to hilarious; of course, when Anne was exhausted or in the middle of something else, it wasn't nearly as funny. What she told Zack was this, "We are going to teach you about time and then we are going to teach you not to mind it. Once you understand the way the rest of the world is going and you can log that in your memory bank, you are free to be whoever you are because you will understand why people get so wound up about certain things and you will make your own priorities."

One of the things Anne is still amazed at with Zack is how he can just feel his whole life. It's like he can just reach within himself and see his future unfold. He fully remembers coming into this world and he describes the entrance into physicality as if he were riding in on a tornado. He remembers how beautiful the non-physical realms are and all of his friends. He knows that he will meet a lot of them here again and many of them aren't born yet. He just knows who he is and where he is going. Anne sees a lot of her role as helping him enjoy physicality and his human body. We have talked about some of the frustrations that Zack has experienced, but it is the enjoyment of being a sensory being on this wonderful planet that Anne believes she can help him with the most. There are many things that can only be experienced in the physical realms and Anne wants Zack to have the joy of playing with every one of them.

*****

Taped to Anne's computer is this Abraham/Hicks quote:

Child of mine, I will never do for you that which I know you can do for yourself. I will never rob you of an opportunity to show yourself your ability and talent. I will see you at all times as the capable, effective, powerful creator that you've come forth to be. And I will stand back as your most avid cheerleading section. But I will not do for you that which you have intended to do for yourself. Anything you need from me, ask. I'm always here to compliment or assist. I am here to encourage your growth, not to justify my experience through you.

Points to Remember

1. Connect with your son or daughter through every phase of the pregnancy.

2. Did you notice how Anne worked with little Zack more as a soul than as a little baby?

3. Even when he was a one and a-half pound baby, Anne knew that Zack was guiding his medical care.

4. Anne and Tom did the best that they could working through the structure of the established medical situation, keeping things positive and not allowing the structure to dictate to them.

5. Anne and Tom have from the beginning recognized that Zack's needs were different, and that many of the things offered by the medical or education communities would not work for him.

6. **Zack came into this world to live his own life, and Anne and Tom trusted him.**

Section 2
Creating and Manifesting

4

Creating our Reality

I've enjoyed studying this topic for more than forty years. Why it isn't taught at every level of school is still beyond me. What could be more important than understanding how we create our reality and that the concept of being a victim is an illusion? This is a complex subject with many layers. In this book, I am introducing to you information that I consider core, as well as some of the subtleties and nuances associated with them. I will extend this information in the next book of this series. If I could have only two things I could teach my children, they would be unconditional love and how to create their reality.

As I said, one of my favorite courses of study over the years is how we create each of our individual realities. This was taught in every ancient school of wisdom, and yet in today's society, it is hardly addressed by the education system. Furthermore, it is one of our most important understandings in order to move into fourth density. This is because it begins to dissolve the illusion of victimhood.

The archetype of victimhood has been with us since our original movement from the non-physical planes of existence into physicality. It is a core wound for humanity. As we begin to understand that we are the creator of our reality and live from that position, this wound heals. We can't be both a creator and a victim simultaneously. The two positions are incompatible.

Many of you might think that these understandings are new, but parts of them actually have been explored in both sports and business for a long period of time: sports in its understanding of sports psychology, and business with its focus on sales and marketing.

Every coach knows the power of a cohesive team: one group mind working together to achieve a common goal. It is amazing what can be accomplished when this kind of team chemistry can be found and nurtured. We also know how fragile this chemistry can be. When you expand this thought, you can begin to see that we are constantly working within group consciousness. Our family and friends are a type of team. Your place of business could easily be seen as such, as well as your community, state and country. Lastly, we have our connection to humanity as a whole.

In sports, all individuals strive to achieve a champion's state of being. This is more than a mindset. It is a state of consciousness. This is the athlete's journey. This is why he or she plays and competes. So much of society focuses on whether or not an individual or team won. Of course, it is fun to win, but that is fleeting. In reality, the outcome of any competition does not matter. The journey does. It is the effort, the preparation, the comradery and the focus that are important. We can always find individuals or teams that are less skilled than we are and consequently win every time if we wished. And what would we learn in the process? If you were simply handed a trophy at the beginning of the season and were told that you just won the championship without ever playing a single game, how would you feel? Pretty empty, don't you think?

Focus is a very important aspect of creation and it is vital to the athlete. When you focus, you are present in the moment and this is far more important than any outcome-based thought. When an athlete is said to be "in the zone," he is so present in the moment that nothing else exists. Every sense is alive and it seems like time slows down. Everything just flows. We are no longer in competition. We are in absolute cooperation. When we are in this state we have the capability of truly reaching our highest potential, and isn't that what it is all about? Literally being "the best that we could be."

66

Business has worked with different aspects of how we create for many years. Books such as Dale Carnegie's *How to Win Friends and Influence People* and Napoleon Hill's *Think and Grow Rich* are classics within the industry. Each emphasizes in its own way the ways that your thoughts and your states of being touch and affect your work. Back in the fifties the concept of "management by objectives" grew in popularity. Its primary focus was to set goals that were measurable and to concentrate heavily on those numbers. As a result, you would see tangible improvement in those areas. This kind of approach, however, did not have a global view; consequently, one area of the business would improve at the expense of another. Also, the theory was based upon cooperation between management and the employees working to achieve their goals. Unfortunately, the goals were frequently dictated by management instead of being cooperative endeavors. System-driven approaches have become popular in recent times, but goal-oriented approaches still have extensive influence.

Network or Relationship Marketing is another type of business approach that utilizes the most positive aspects of how your thoughts create reality. This style of marketing really focuses on self-improvement and self-realization. One of my favorite sayings used in Network Marketing is this...

The greatest benefit of being involved in Network Marketing isn't what you get by being involved. The greatest benefit is what you become.

My point in mentioning how sports and businesses have utilized some of these concepts is to understand that the way thoughts and states of being create is not a new idea. It has been around for a long time, just under different labels. Also, many areas of society wish to control you and the rest of the populace. Their tool of choice is fear. If you can be conditioned to believe that you have no control of your life, then you have to look outside yourself for that control, and when you do, they win at your expense. How much of advertising is designed to create fear? What about all the information that comes from various governmental agencies? How about all the fear-mongering by the pharmaceutical companies? It goes on and on.

Think how life might be for you if you eliminated fear from your life. Feels pretty good, doesn't it?

What about happiness? Did you know that your current circumstance in life is only a ten percent indicator of your level of happiness? That's right. Rich, poor, healthy or ill, your happiness is a choice. And yet so much of the conditioning in society is designed to convince you that you will be happy only if your circumstances change. But what if you decided to be happy first? Shawn Achor, a Harvard positive psychologist, has compiled a lot of research in this area in his two books, *The Happiness Advantage* and *Before Happiness*. The research findings are quite profound. Your performance in virtually every area of life improves when you are happy versus being unhappy or in a neutral state. Your mind works faster. You see more options to problems that lie before you. Your ability to perform any task improves and, most importantly, you become healthier.

Shifting from Doing to Being

As I've mentioned before, everything is energy, which means we are vibrational beings living in a vibrational universe. This is one of the primary messages that Esther and Jerry Hicks have been conveying with the Abraham material for more than thirty years, and it is one of the most important concepts that you as a parent and individual need to incorporate into your life. As I mentioned previously, we are shifting from **doing to living**. Another way of saying this is that we are shifting from **doing to being**. We are all creators. Everything that occurs in our lives, we have created or co-created with our vibration and our choices. Just because you do not know on a conscious level why something has occurred doesn't mean that you didn't create it. No matter how tragic, no matter how dramatic, on *some level* we have created every experience that we have had on this planet. For the average person, eighty five percent of their actions come from a habit or some other unconscious action.

Some things we even put in motion before we are born. We all create a life plan prior to our birth and within it are many of the life events that we wish to experience. In my work, I've seen examples of individuals that had life lessons play out over five, ten, and even twenty different lifetimes. The subtlety around this, however, is that even though you might have set up this experience prior to your incarnation, how you reacted in the scene was entirely up to you in the moment.

Take something that can be very traumatic, such as cancer. On a conscious level, the individual didn't wake up one morning and say, "I think I would like to experience cancer today." That is absurd, and yet he or she still created it. However, this is not how society has conditioned you to see it. You are trained to see yourself as a victim. Think back on all the movies and TV shows you might have seen. Have you ever seen an individual in any media ever question how he or she created some drama the show was portraying? Of course not, it ruins the hero's journey formula. They love to have a hero, a villain and a victim play out the various story lines. This, however, is not self-realization.

So, if I am the creator of the cancer in my body, how did I go about doing this? First of all, there are many different ways that cancer can be creating within one's body. One of the most common is that it represents unhealed emotional energy that has festered in the body over time. Heal this emotional energy and the cancer will also be healed. It could even be created by a single emotional trauma. Long-term stress can certainly cause cancer; consequently, it would be the culmination of a thousand different choices over many years. Every situation is different, and this is the problem that modern science and traditional medicine have. They want to see something like cancer as having a single physical cause and this just isn't the case. We exist on many different levels and we create from all of them.

I've spent a lifetime looking at the myriad events that have happened in my life and attempted to understand how they were created. In every instance, I was given an understanding that made complete sense. I call it "looking behind the curtain" (in reference to The Wizard of Oz). Understanding the interrelationship of how our energy interacts with the universe is vital if you are ever going to move away from the old paradigms and out of Separation consciousness. Everyone will say they want to lead happier and healthier lives, but will they do the work necessary to make the changes? We love to take credit for all the wonderful things that occur in our lives, but all too often see ourselves as victims if something difficult occurs. When we change our perspective and look for the gifts in every circumstance, and what we are to learn in each instance, then we start disconnecting from the victim paradigm. Whether something is good, bad, right or wrong is always based on a perspective and a judgment. Our human perspective is so limited versus that of our soul or higher self.

For many of us, part of the problem with understanding that our thoughts create our reality has always been the time delay in our manifestations. Because we are such spiritual children, we collectively put a protective veil in position thousands of years ago. This veil was designed to slow down our creations. The problem was not about the level of good or happiness that existed in society, but the level of fear. Fear, as we know, is a tremendously powerful emotion and its manifestations can be very destructive. At any point in time, whatever it is that you are focusing on is expanding and being drawn to you. If the predominant vibration coming from you is fearful and the universe is complying with your request, then you are creating an experience with a like vibration to that fear, and I can assure you this won't be fun. The veil slowed the creation process down because we weren't ready for instant manifestations and we still aren't. However, in 2012, we as a collective took a huge step forward and dissolved the largest of these veils. In essence, we took the training wheels off the bicycle. As a result, we are manifesting more than one hundred times faster than previously. I hope you are ready because this is the new reality that we are living in.

Understanding how your thoughts and your states of being create has now been taken to a whole new level of importance.

In December 2012, a lot of people were focused on the ending of the Mayan Calendar. Certainly the ending of that twenty five thousand year cycle was very important but this wasn't all that was taking place. Mother Earth also moved fully into her fourth density body. For us to move with her, the veils of third density had to begin to dissolve.

I've studied how thoughts create realities for more than fourty years. The subtleties and nuances of the material still amaze me. The best material I could offer you as a new person dipping your toes into the subject for the first time would be the channeled information that Esther Hicks has brought forth. Also, the movie *The Secret* is an excellent presentation of the basics and was based on the Abraham/Hicks material. Dr. Wayne Dyer, Tony Robbins, Jim Rohn and many others have contributed excellent substance on the subject. Find the one that resonates with you and have fun with wherever it takes you. If you like a more scientific style of information, you may enjoy Shawn Achor's books or those written by other positive psychologists.

As excellent as these mentioned materials are, I still consider most of them basic. The reason is simple: most of society's needs are at this level. For those of you that are ready for more, check out Dr. Joe Dispenza. I have loved studying with Dr. Joe at his workshops. His story is a fascinating one.

Dr. Joe was a chiropractor. When he was in his twenties, he was competing in a triathlon and was on the bicycle portion of the competition. An old lady did not see the bikers or the policeman stopping traffic. As Dr. Joe rounded the turn, he was hit by her car, which was going forty five miles an hour, and he was dragged on the pavement for some distance before she finally brought the car to a stop. Dr. Joe suffered six broken vertebrae in the accident. Over the next two days, three different teams of doctors looked at his case and each recommended surgically placing rods in his back around the spinal cord. Of course, the consequence of that would be possible paralysis and never walking again. Somehow, Dr. Joe found it within himself to refuse the surgeries. Several days later, after his discharge, he was moved to a friend's apartment where he lay in bed immobile, his fate unknown.

Over the next three months, Dr. Joe spent every moment that he could visualizing a healthy spine. As a chiropractor he knew every inch of the spine and would draw it over and over in his mind. He had to fully immerse himself in the experience, and it was one of the hardest things he had ever done because all the questioning and all the negativity had to be cleared from his mind. He had to become, within his mind, a man with a healthy spine and the other injured man had to disappear. The injured Dr. Joe could not exist within the new hologram, only the healthy one. It took him over two months before he was able to draw his spine fully in one meditation without any extraneous thoughts or fears intruding. Imagine all the lonely nights and fears he must have been dealing with. And yet at the end of three months, Dr. Joe, completely healed, walked out of his friend's apartment and into a life of study on how thoughts and our states of being create realities. How thoughts can affect one's health and happiness regardless of external circumstances. His key to the whole process: "*...In order to create by thought alone, you must become thought alone.*" This may sound simple but don't be deceived. To attain this state it takes training, practice and determination.

Core Understandings

What Dr. Joe did was very advanced. I like to call it "graduate school" manifesting. It is something all of us can achieve but most of us have never worked at that level. So, just like in school most of us don't go from elementary school right to grad school. We have to master the basics before we are ready for more. It is one thing to have the understandings and knowledge of these basics at a mental level. I want you to live them and move them to an experiential level. That's when you really begin to own them.

- You are a creator.
- You are manifesting all the time whether you are trying to or not. The laws of attraction are constantly at work around and through you. The concepts are very simple, but it is the nuances that move them from being just information for the brain to living experiences within your reality.
- One of the simplest phrases to always keep in mind is that *"what you focus on expands."*
- You must become that which you are wishing to attract to yourself.

What this last statement is referring to is the fact that in order to manifest something in the physical reality you'll be moving from something you do not have and desiring something else. It could be anything. What most people do not fully understand is that you must become the new energy regardless of the conditions around you. Most of society has been conditioned to live within the mindset of, "I'll be happy when…." But the universe doesn't work that way. The universe sends to you the energy that you are putting out. Hence the saying, "Fake it 'til you make it."

Take abundance for example. Abundance consciousness is about living abundantly on every level of your life. It is not just about having additional money in your bank account, although that would certainly be nice. Your job would be to live abundantly in everything you do. But we sabotage ourselves in so many ways and normally don't even recognize it. How many times have you said, "…I can't afford that," or as my mother used to say, "money doesn't grow on trees." Thoughts of lack and limitation will constantly undermine your abundance consciousness, and for every step forward you take one backward. In so doing, you become frustrated and assume that nothing will ever change. We look outside ourselves and see ourselves as victims of our circumstances.

Most people become fixated on finance as abundance and don't ever take into account other ways that we can be abundant that don't cost a single cent. We can be abundant in loving and caring for others. We can be abundant in the gift of our smile. We can share joy with everyone we come across. We can be abundant in the giving of our gifts and talents, whatever they may be. Abundance is an energy and a vibration that the universe recognizes. It is not just money.

Conscious living requires you to be diligent in your focus. You have to become aware of **you**. Your patterns, your beliefs, what you are creating and what you have created in the past. If it is in your life, you created it. For most people, eighty-five percent of what they do in their day-to-day lives is controlled by patterns from the subconscious mind. Think about it: eighty-five percent. Considering that our subconscious is working with old patterns, it is amazing that we can get anything new created. And yet the power of pure thought is truly remarkable. Here is a piece from Esther Hicks and Abraham on what you can accomplish in as little as sixty eight seconds.

Abraham/Esther Hicks Sixty Eight Seconds of Pure Thought

People will say to us, "I can't just go on the beach and meditate," or, "I can't stop what I'm doing and just imagine. I have children to feed or dishes to wash or things to do." And we say, "We are not encouraging you to stop the action part of your life. We are encouraging you to act just a little bit less and that you envision just a little bit more. What we would like to say to you is that there is power in lining up energy the likes of which in your action orientation you don't really know. "

*When you find a thought and you hold that thought purely for as little as seventeen seconds, now there is a lot of power in the word **pure**. Because **pure** means a thought that is not contradicted. When you find a thought of something* *you wanted and you hold that purely by imagining it, pretending it, remembering something like it, using it... When you hold that thought for as little as seventeen seconds, another thought on the same vibration equivalence, because of the Law of Attraction, joins it. And when those two thoughts come together there is an explosion of energy. So in order to give you an idea of the power, we would say to you that when that first seventeen seconds joins the equivalent thought, there is an energy expansion equivalent of two thousand action hours. That is huge. When you cross the next seventeen second mark, the expression of energy is ten times the first. Twenty-thousand action hours just by walking across that next mark. When you hold it for the third sequence of seventeen seconds... Another ten times... Each time there is another seventeen seconds of non-contradiction, the thought catapults into a whole new level. So that sixty eight seconds of pure thought have huge action consequences. That's why we say, "one who is connected to Source is many, many, many, many times more powerful than one who is not, because there is no self-defeating that is going on," you see.*

As you can see there is incredible power when we're focused and present in the moment. Abraham also mentions another very important point. When you are focused on making a change and have decided to do some process, the results will diminish significantly. The reason for this is that your energy or your thoughts are now residing in both places — where you are now and where you want to go — and they are canceling each other out. You are not holding a pure thought in this instance. Similar problems occur when your subconscious mind and conscious mind are not in sync with one another. It has the same type of effect.

When you enter into a visualization for the *pleasure of the visualization* you avoid this pitfall. In hypnotherapy, we create visualizations similar to this all the time. It's an excellent technique to create new patterns within the mind as well as send out specific vibrations to the universe. We want our client to be fully immersed in the scene that we are creating for them. Abraham uses a movie as a great analogy.

> When you go to a movie, you don't say to your friends, "I'm going to this movie because it's about things I want to live and I think if I go watch the movie I'll vibrate like the movie is vibrating and then the universe will yield to me." Although that's not a bad way of approaching a movie.

Most people go to the movies for entertainment. That is their intention. And yet while they're there they become immersed in the scenes of the movie and in doing so their vibration syncs to that of the movie. So for two and a half hours without even trying, you are sending a specific vibration out into the universe. There is no effort involved. You are merely immersed in the moment. Don't visualize to make something happen. Visualize for the pleasure of visualizing. You want to take every opportunity to create your desired vibration within your being just for the sake of feeling that energy.

Kids have played games within their minds for thousands of years. In modern times, they might see themselves playing in the World Series of baseball and it's the bottom of the ninth and they are the batter with a chance to drive in the winning run. They have a blast envisioning themselves getting the winning hit or scoring the winning run. A young golfer does the same, playing games in his or her mind as they stand over a putt and say to themselves that if they make this putt they win the Masters or perhaps the U.S. Open. As you play these games you begin to build networks of neurons within your brain. But most importantly, you are sending vibrations out into the universe and every seventeen seconds of pure thought increases the power of these thoughts exponentially.

Prayer, when it comes from the thought that you lack something, can have all the same problems that we are describing here. Prayer from a place of gratitude, however, creates the energy that we are looking for.

Inelia Benz – Connecting with the Spirit of Money

Inelia Benz also has a wonderful guided meditation on connecting with the spirit of money that illustrates some of these concepts, and I would like to share it with you. This is from her YouTube video on connecting with the spirit of money.

Connecting with the Spirit of Money

So many people have a lot of problems attracting money into their lives. It has been a strong pattern in many areas of society. The "why" is unimportant for our purposes. However, you will have to work through your own personal blocks that are creating this particular problem in your life. This exercise will help you identify your blocks and hopefully help to heal them.

*After you learn this exercise you really need to do it once or twice a day, preferably after you have done your meditation. The most important thing about money that you need to understand is that it is an **energy being**. It is **alive**. Think of it as an **elemental**. A very powerful, very important elemental. I would say that it is probably the most important elemental in your life today. That, of course, is because of the nature of the world we are living in. Especially if you are living in a Western country where you need money to survive. Money allows you to do the most basic things such as drinking fresh water, having a place to live, having clothes on your body, being able to express yourself creatively, eating every day. The most basic things in life come with your exchange of money, therefore, it is extremely important. Another aspect of money that I'd like you to understand is that money is not evil. Some people use money in a negative way but the money itself has nothing negative about it. Once you identify and connect* *with the energy of money you will see it for yourself. It's all inclusive. It's creative. It's nurturing. It's warm. It's beautiful and I want you to be able to experience this.*

For this exercise, you're going to need some money to hold. Notes are better than coins, but if you don't have any at the moment, coins will do. The next time try to have the notes – and the bigger the note the better.

➢ Put the note between your two palms resting gently in front of you. It is going to look a little bit like you are praying, but your hands are going to be resting forward so that they are nice and comfortable.

➢ It is really important during this exercise that you do not ask for stuff. I've noticed that there is a tendency for somebody when they're contacting money or when they feel that they are starting to contact money, to ask for things. Oh, I want a new car. I want the new job. I want more money for food. I want... Whatever. Don't do that.

➢ Think of it like you are going to make a new friend. And if you're going to make a new friend you aren't going to start by asking them for stuff. What we are going to do first is to get acquainted with the energy of money and then we're going to allow it to express itself in our energy field. That is all we are going to do right now.

➢ So hold money between your palms and clear your mind.

➢ Next, we are going to feel the note. Just feel it. Feel it between your palms. Allow it to be there. Soon it is going to start feeling warm. Feel the lovely warmth coming out of it. This is the first signature that you are going to identify about money. That it is warm.

> I want you to say "hi." And tell it that you allow it to express itself to you, and then just listen. Quiet your mind and listen. See if any images or any thoughts come to your mind and allow that to happen.

> The first time I did this I actually got an image of my mother pulling a note away from me, away from my mouth and rushing me to the bathroom; washing my mouth out and telling me how dirty money was. And I should never put money in my mouth. And that I should always wash my hands after touching money. Obviously, it shocked me and it caused a huge block because I could not allow money into my life. You know. I couldn't allow money to touch me, it was dirty. I was actually quite surprised when I saw that image. I had completely forgotten about it. So I thanked it and I released it. And if you're getting any sort of negative feedback from this exercise, that's all you have to do. Just thank the image, the feelings, or blocks and release them. They are coming up now so you can release them.

> It took me a few weeks to work through several blocks and eventually I was able to just sit there and allow money to express itself to me. The next stage is to allow it into your energy field. Your energy field is your life, it's you. It's your body, your thoughts, your emotions, your reality. So

once you receive a good positive feedback from money and you are allowing it to express itself to you, completely and utterly, I want you to ask it to come into your life. To come into your energy field. I can tell you it's going to be extremely happy to do so because money likes nothing better than to be plentiful in your life. That's the only way it can express itself. To be plentiful. To be in every aspect of your life.

➢ So how this translates on a practical level is basically you let the note between your hands become warm. You allow it to become warm. And you allow that warmth to grow and to encompass you. To come into your life. The flow of it and the love of it.

➢ The signature you will find is extremely similar to that of Mother Earth because they are one and the same. Welcome it, embrace it.

➢ After you are done, say "thank you" to the elemental of money for having expressed itself fully to you. Open your eyes if they were closed and put your money away. Remember to do this exercise at least once a day.

What you will consistently see in any material about how we create is that you must *become* the energy that you are trying to create. And the easiest way to do that is by creating an alternate reality within your mind and live that reality every chance you get. Eventually, that new perspective becomes more dominant than your previous one and your reality changes in the process.

Scientists have been fascinated for years by how the mind does not see any difference between a fully immersed visualization and an actual experience. The same neuron sequences fire in your brain. The same muscle actuations trigger within your body, and even chemicals and hormones begin to be signaled by your brain. What Abraham is attempting to convey is that within your visualization or meditation you must play in the new energies and exclude the former. When you meditate with the purpose of shifting, you are still holding on to both vibrations simultaneously. Play with the new energies, thoughts and emotions just for the sake of being in that energy.

Victimhood

The archetype of victimhood has been around for thousands of years, and yet within the understanding that we are all divine creators, the idea of being a victim dissolves away. You can't be both. You are either one or the other. Being a victim is based on the thought that the individual was innocent within a particular scene. But as an infinite soul you are in touch with everything, on every level, so how could you be separate from the choices and vibrations that placed you within a particular experience? I realize that most of society produces about eight five percent of their creations *unconsciously*. That doesn't mean that we aren't capable of improving. We can move to the point where all of us are living examples of conscious creation.

We are creators of our reality, and yet we still judge individuals as victims within particular experiences just because we don't know how or why they participated or created them. Every event we create has a purpose on some level. The reasons are infinite. We all have within us the Akashic Records the records of every lifetime that we have ever lived and with the correct level of integrity we can access them.

The Akashic Records or "The Book of Life" can be equated
to the universe's super computer system. It is this system

81

that acts as the central storehouse of all information for every individual who has ever lived upon the earth. More than just a reservoir of events, the Akashic Records contain every deed, word, feeling, thought and intent that has ever occurred at any time in the history of the world. Much more than simply a memory storehouse, however, these Akashic Records are interactive in that they have a tremendous influence on our everyday lives, our relationships, our feelings and belief systems, and the potential realities we draw toward us.
(Edgar Cayce)

Within the records, we have our Life chart. It contains all we have chosen to experience in this lifetime, as well as all the soul contracts that we have put in place. By and by we are gaining access to this level of information, but only to the extent that it will benefit that which we are to learn and experience on Earth. I had the pleasure of having my good friend Dr. Anthony Kennedy access the records of each of my children when they were in their late teens. I found the information to be very helpful with some of the decisions we were facing as the kids were entering early adulthood. We all would like to know why we are here and what our soul's purpose is. It certainly makes college and other education choices easier.

Equally interesting can be the information that you can find as to how or why you participated in a particular life event. I've looked at every kind of experience you can imagine and without a doubt, there is always a reason, a lesson, and a gift within each and every one. Just knowing this can begin to open you up to new perspectives. Sometimes I am able to see the gifts and lessons myself, and other times I'm not. Sometimes I need a different perspective in order to see the value in a particular experience. I just keep looking until I find something that feels right to me.

One of my favorite examples to share is that of the actor Christopher Reeves. He starred in several movies as Superman. He was six foot three inches tall and two hundred twenty five pounds and handsome. The world was his oyster. He had a horseback riding accident and wound up spending the rest of his life in a wheelchair. He helped and inspired far more people as a quadriplegic than he ever did as an actor. If I were to cure Christopher's body and restore his old life to him, would I be doing him a service or a disservice? I have no doubt that on a soul level Christopher had amazing growth through his difficult experience. Normally, only very advanced souls will take on this level of difficulty. And yet would you believe that there are more souls on the other side that would like to come into a lifetime on Earth with a handicapped body than there are opportunities available?

I studied for several years with Dolores Cannon. She pioneered what she called the Quantum Healing Hypnosis Technique (QHHT). This technique uses deep trance hypnosis to help an individual connect more fully with their higher levels of consciousness. This higher level knows everything about each one of us, and by accessing it we are often provided with answers to some of our most troubling questions. Also, all forms of healing have been demonstrated within this technique. This brings me back to the issue of why you as an individual created a particular disease, injury or other experience. When you have learned what you were to learn, then frequently what I call the Superconscious can heal or help heal an individual on the spot. But what if you haven't looked within at the experience? Let's say that you had - deep-seated anger toward an individual and you refused to let it go or to forgive that person. Do you think your Superconscious will deem that it is in your best interest to heal your created condition? Of course not.

What I have found in my experience is that any condition **can** be healed as long as the individual does not have a soul contract connected with the situation preventing the healing. This restriction even applied to Jesus. Normally, individuals that can access this level of healing can also access the records, and as such, know more fully what is going on with the individual and how they can be of assistance. A soul-level contract is part of our Free Will Choice and

83

cannot be violated. The fun part of all of this is that as our consciousness continues to shift, more and more of us are able to connect with these levels of energy ourselves.

One last note about QHHT. Just because something can be cured does not necessarily mean that it will be. Every situation is unique and all a QHHT practitioner provides is a deeper connection with your Superconscious by helping you get your analytical mind out of the way. All of us can work with this level of consciousness with practice. Unfortunately, most of us do not take the time to quiet the mind to the level where we can hear that which is attempting to be conveyed. Still, recognizing that this is available to us is always a first step.

Points to Remember

1. When we live from the understanding that we are the creators of our reality, the archetype of victimhood then is allowed to heal.

2. The current circumstances in your life are only a ten percent indicator of your happiness.

3. We are vibrational beings living in a vibrational universe.

4. We are shifting from **doing** to **being**.

5. What you focus on expands.

6. In 2012, we as a collective removed our largest veil that was slowing down our manifestations. We are now creating our positive thoughts and our fear one hundred times faster than before.

7. You must become that which you desire to attract to yourself.

8. Seventeen seconds of pure thought is the equivalent of two thousand action hours. Sixty eight seconds of pure thought equates to two million action hours.

9. Whether something is good, bad, right or wrong is always based on a perspective and a judgment.

5

Gratitude

Most people have some understanding that gratitude is very helpful in their lives. Few people, however, understand how vital it is in receiving your manifestations. This rare chapter gives you a peek behind the curtain and shows you what is actually occurring when you enter this state, and how paying your gratitude forward is vital to your creations.

As we learn more about creating and manifesting, we quickly find that setting goals and working hard creates a mixed bag of results. If we don't believe that we are going to achieve something, all the hard work and struggle won't get it done. You have to believe it, not just at the conscious level but at the subconscious as well. Frequently, though, we have left the belief part out of what we have told our children so we have statements and thoughts like this:

If your mind can conceive it, you can achieve it.

The more accurate saying is:

That which your mind can conceive and believe you can achieve.

This brings us to the energy of trust of ourselves, trust of our soul, and trust of our Source. As you can imagine, there are a lot of potholes we can fall into along the way, and normally they are of our own making. So perhaps a better understanding of what is going on behind the scenes might help in this area.

Virtually every creation that you have ever wanted, ever desired on any level, already exists for you within the time continuum. All the people, situations and occurrences that will greet you this year are already positioned there for you. Patiently waiting for you to arrive. They are already written into the fibers of your own being.

This takes place the moment you **make any choice**. These two points, the activated choice and the completion energy, are linked together. Like two giant etheric magnets, they beckon to each other. When the physical aspect that is you is finally willing and aligns with the energetic aspect of you, then the manifestation is seen in the physical reality.

However, because of our level of trust within ourselves, the pattern we normally see is quite different. Regardless of where we are in this area, the fact is, the moment we make a choice, any choice, it is granted energetically. Then, due to our unreadiness to receive the result into our life, the energy that completes the manifestation of our choice is positioned in the time continuum just ahead of where we are now. In essence, you are giving yourself a grace period to allow yourself to be able to receive that which you desire. As you move through your life and come to a time where one of these magnetic points rests, even if you're not yet in alignment with it, the opportunity is not lost. The points and their connections are simply moved by your soul to a later position within the continuum, to a time where you would have embraced the level of trust necessary to allow the full presentation of your chosen desire. In this way, you miss no opportunity. Each is simply shifted forward again and again until you are ready to receive it.

Think back to how many times you were on the verge of getting what you had worked so hard to achieve. Then in the next day, week or month the energy just seemed to dissipate. Did you feel that your desired goal was slipping through your fingers and disappearing as well? This is typically followed by disappointment. What is most derailing to your life, however, is that the energy of disappointment is generally inwardly directed. Your mind revisits all the times that you failed in the past and you begin to second-guess yourself. What did I do? What did I not do? Could I have done more? Was I worthy of this? All the while your goal was literally right at your fingertips. All that has to be done at that pivotal moment is to say "**yes**" to yourself at your deepest level. Say "**yes**" and let your energy and physical being connect with that which is already given.

Sometimes when you get close to your goal, you may experience a wave of sadness. Considering how close you are to your desired intention, your emotional reaction can be pretty confusing for you. What has occurred is that another part of the mind has realized that the process of this particular acquisition is complete. Then, the level of the mind that has always been committed to the chase falls into a state of grief. There is nothing more for it to stretch or reach for. The sadness experienced is a result of that level of the mind feeling displaced and losing its value or focus. I've seen this many times in my own life. Even when you complete your project and you feel the joy of that accomplishment, there can be a permeating sadness simultaneously. Again, I invite you to say "yes" and offer gratitude to yourself. Say "yes" to the sadness, but not in a manner where you are acquiescing to its assumptions, but rather as a clear and pure acknowledgment that the sadness exists. This "yes" is not agreeing or disagreeing with the energy of sadness. What it is doing is comforting the mind and letting it know that it was heard.

Thank you can also be focused toward the mind. It is a clear and simple expression of gratitude for the mind having shared its current perspective with you. At times this will immediately dissolve the veil of sadness, allowing you to know the thought which motivated it. At other times, the sadness might dissipate without you having an awareness of its origin. And that is okay because the reason for the emotion is irrelevant. All that does matter is that the mind found complete comfort in just being heard and acknowledged. (Michaels, 2005)

Additionally, your gratitude in situations like this is offered to whatever the immediate future is bringing. You do this without classifying what that future is, only the absolute assurance that it is being delivered as a service to you and your life. In doing so, you don't obstruct what is flowing into your life at that moment. Everything you do receive at any time is the end result of combining the choices of the many levels of your human self and your soul, which always desires for you the most expansive, supportive experiences available.

Your manifestations and choices can come from many levels of your being; it is important to recognize that we still have free will. Our entire universe is based on this concept. It is just that all of our manifestations are not necessarily centered within our conscious mind. **As we share gratitude forward, we begin to stabilize ourselves in the absolute awareness that everything we experience was and is chosen.** This is one of the reasons hope is so powerful. As each of us goes about our days, we find that we are calmer and more balanced. As we make our choices more and more from this calm, nurturing space, it allows the creation points within our personal energy field to connect with those within the time continuum far more consciously and more spontaneously.

Creating and manifesting is not just about doing. It isn't about setting goals and then by some force of will doing something until the energies are hammered into place. It is much more like the yin and yang.

Yang	Yin
Sun	Moon
Light	Dark
Heaven	Earth
Active	Passive
Fire	Water
Above	Below
Heat	Cold

Yes, choices must be made and actions taken but if you aren't in a state of receivership and allowing, nothing will come to pass. Your ability to allow and receive is just as important to nurture as your ability to take action. In many ways, I see the art of allowing as the secret sauce in this recipe of manifestation, and gratitude is its secret ingredient.

As far as I'm concerned, any practice of gratitude is beneficial. You can begin dinner by sharing with your family three things you are grateful for that happened during the day. You might even describe acts of kindness or compassion you observed or even better, those you participated in. Some people like to journal. As such, you could write down each night before going to bed the same types of thoughts and occurrences. You can also journal about people. You can do this with your family, friends or anyone whom you choose. You simply write down something that you are grateful for in regard to this individual. Try to come up with something new each time. So often people in society see a small aspect of someone that they don't like and this becomes their point of focus. When you are constantly looking for something to be grateful for, your entire circuitry within your brain begins to shift and change. The key in all of these is to use different thoughts each day, and in so doing your brain searches more in your environment for gratitude.

Gratitude is one of the greatest gifts you can offer another. When expressed generously and freely, gratitude opens our hearts more fully than any other emotion. As we open our hearts through the expression of sincere gratitude, this openness spreads out through our entire physical, mental, emotional and energetic bodies. Gratitude, as one of the faces of love, has the power to gently and naturally open every cell in your body, every synapse within your brain, every connector within your energy and every wave within your emotions into an authentic transparent state. This is transparency with our true self, the all of who we are. This also means that as we live from a state of gratitude, each magnetic connection point within our being is spontaneously and directly linked to the magnetic connection points within the time continuum. We begin to walk seamlessly and effortlessly into the positions where our choices are fulfilled in the most complete manner.

Offering gratitude in any direction is not exclusively a state of giving. You are not just offering. Each act of gratitude triggers your mind, body, emotions and energy to relax into an expansive self-openness, which settles your entire being more completely in the moment. As you offer gratitude in any direction, you also receive a return of the energy you are offering. Even more exciting is the way in which this innate boomerang effect settles the energetic return deeply within your being, creating greater inward expansion. And this is only part of the magic activated in a moment. Each time you open wholly through the transparent offering of gratitude, even without realizing it, you initiate every other energy of enhancement, support, generosity, and personal validation that has been offered by any person, at any time, to flood into your being. Each of us carries **un-activated** energies of generosity and appreciation that were at one time presented in our direction but **have not yet** been fully embraced. Just because we didn't receive them when they were given does not mean they have been lost forever. They are quietly spiraling through the outer reaches of our energy until such time as we invite them in. Offering gratitude is a passive and yet extremely powerful means of allowing such energies to now become a part of all that is uplifting. This essentially means that *gratitude places each of us in our greatest position of receptivity.*

It has been humorous to look at the myriad ways in which each of us blocks our own ability to receive. My mother was an extremely hard-working woman. My dad died when I was only eight and she raised four of us by herself back in the 60s. Mother loved to give, but she had a very self-effacing way of accepting gifts when they came her way. I'll never forget her little pet phrase: *"Oh you shouldn't have..."*

Words are powerful and your body believes every one of them.

Think of how much more Mother might have received had she accepted all the returning kindnesses that she had extended to others if she had enthusiastically just said **thank you**. I know she was trying in her own way to be humble and thank them for their effort, but our words do matter. They carry very specific energies and vibrations. We all have subtle ways in which we sabotage ourselves. The more each of us becomes aware and transparent with the deeper levels of our own being, the more we will see for ourselves where the energy of gratitude can assist us. The universe isn't putting blocks in our way, we are.

Gratitude is one way to really help
us begin to get out of our own way.

Think for a moment about the practice of doing random gifts of kindness and how that plays into everything we're talking about.

When we offer a random gift, a flow of energy much like the shape of the infinity symbol ∞ opens up between you and the other individual. A combination of gifting and receiving opens up. This is wonderful by itself, but there is more. Your subconscious begins to be reprogrammed to accept the understandings that gifts or energy can come from anywhere. You don't have to do everything. The universe helps as well, but you do have to allow it.

As you practice gratitude in every opportunity your life provides, be aware of what you are feeling. Too often people move into a space of feeling indebted when support is offered. This obviously can stifle the flow of energy. It disallows the blessing's ability to saturate your being and eliminates your ability to be in unabashed gratitude. So, just say **thank you** from a place devoid of indebtedness and then relax and receive fully.

As you are well aware, there is no energy which can offer the level of healing that simple, unstructured love delivers. Subsequently, as you continue playing with **love's most potent expression**, *gratitude*, you will observe an ever- growing comfort with transparency, both inwardly and outwardly expressed. There may be occasions when you feel yourself becoming giddy during the experience. This is the true joy of your being flowing in tremendous freedom. On occasion, you may even receive a call from a loved one either during or immediately after playing in the vast well of gratitude and transparency. Without realizing so, they are responding to the love you are sending experienced through the link of ever-present connectedness that each and every one of us on this planet and beyond share.

It is easy for most people to understand the level that gratitude plays in any given moment but still struggle with the concept of paying gratitude forward. Just as we can reactivate energies and extend gratitude to individuals and situations from our past, we can equally do the same with future energy. Of course, in the case of future blessings, you don't know from whence they will come. Therefore, instead of extending gratitude toward a particular individual, situation, or circumstance, you can **extend the gratitude into the universe**. As you do this, fully knowing that every being that exists is ever-connected, the one positioned to bring you blessings at some future point will most assuredly receive the gift of your gratitude. Additionally, by offering the energy directly to the universe, it will ease the act of remaining in the present moment. Or, if you prefer, you can **extend your gratefulness toward the time continuum**. The benefit of this approach is that, again, you are able to remain steadfast within the moment. As you offer gratitude to the time continuum, the love you are passing forward will naturally spiral along the rhythms of the continuum until meeting with the precise point connected to the blessings you are set to receive.

So, why would you want to offer gratitude for that which has not yet entered your personal reality? Several reasons. **One is that great power and wisdom lives and breathes within the willingness to *be*: *just being* grateful for what you do not now know and for gratitude around the fact that you don't know.** This is centered on one of our greatest fears, which is the "fear of the unknown." This fear hinders so many of our creations. Our minds wrestle against proceeding forward without absolute assurance that the future will meet with our, or more specifically, its, approval. Of course, this is based in control, which is propelled by a lack of trust on so many levels. I am inviting you to understand that gratitude for that which is unknown is the mental, emotional and energetic commitment to acknowledging that all which is life- enhancing will be revealed as it does manifest into your life, and also to know **that it will** manifest into your life. In fact, it is doing so even in this moment. Furthermore, expressing gratitude for that which is not yet known is the actualization of all levels of trust within your being and through all that is.

As you offer gratitude to the future, which is based on the assurance of blessings continuing, you are repeatedly stating to yourself that you are never without support and that you are always in flow with the universe as well as with Source's generosity. Further, you are stabilizing within yourself vast expressions of trust—that you are open to receiving gifts and wonders. Moreover, as you offer gratitude for future blessings, you are sharing unwavering assurance with your mind, body and spirit that the future is a given, that, without question, it will be a wondrous adventure. This action, in and of itself, will be the most powerful healing you have ever offered to your mind and emotions. You see, spiraling gratitude forward in time establishes a prevailing wave of higher vibrational loving presence that will dissolve any lingering stories which have plagued you at any time within your life. All the old and outdated waves of doubt will be replaced with a pathway of gentleness, along which you will be able to proceed throughout all your future days.

As we bring more gratitude into our being, we can't help but activate the Law of Attraction within us. Our minds begin to see the level of blessings that we have in the current moment as well as those that have occurred in the past. As each of these energies is felt, our natural magnetic attraction to more of the same occurs, and our connections to those points that we have placed within our timeline naturally become stronger. Now realize that as you flow with life in the spirit of gratitude (and gratitude is a living spirit), you will find yourself spontaneously noticing how much more you have had in many past moments. This is done without realizing the expansion.

94

When you weave gratitude through your mind, body and emotions—as a consistent state of being, of expression, of love in movement—the tapestry you are creating becomes a bold, enlivened presentation of your most authentic self. And remember as you play with this in your future days, it is not just a mantra. Play with Gratitude. Dance spontaneously when you feel it rolling through you. Sing it when you are so inspired and can no longer contain the energy. Gratitude has, and is, passion, laughter and joyousness. **It carries within it the power to inspire beyond imagination.** So live your personal version of being fully alive with the presence of gratitude.

Points to Remember

1. That which your mind can conceive and
    believe you can achieve.

2. Virtually every creation that you have ever
    wanted, ever desired on any level, already
    exists for you within the time continuum.

3. As we share gratitude forward, we begin
    to stabilize ourselves in the absolute
    awareness that everything we experience
    was and is chosen.

4. Choices must be made and actions taken,
    but if you aren't in a state of receivership
    and allowing, nothing will come to pass.

5. Gratitude places each of us in our greatest
    position of receptivity.

6

The Art of Worrying

The Law of Attraction is really very simple. What you focus on expands. So why on earth do we keep focusing on what we don't want to have occur?

One of the concepts I have worked with for years has to do with the concept of holding the highest image possible of any of my children instead of society's old habit of worrying. Each individual comes into a lifetime with different challenges they have set up for themselves. They also have the capabilities to handle these challenges regardless of how difficult they might be. The energy that we add to this mix can make a big difference. The choice is yours.

Any discussion on how thoughts create must include an understanding of what you are really doing when you are worrying about your child or grandchild. Worrying has been with us for a long time. Not only is it considered socially acceptable, but most parents, if they do not worry, might be considered bad parents by their peers. Society today has construed worrying as caring and the two are very, very different. Worrying is actually a fear of a possible future outcome that we project toward our children. We are putting our energy into exactly what we don't want to have happen. It is like screaming at the universe that you have a fear in a specific area and that you would like to have an experience around it so you can address it. And because fears carry a lot of emotion with them, it is quite possible that you are putting a lot of negative energy into your concern.

The universe also has the ability within our manifestations to create not only what we focus on, but also bring to us experiences that are of a similar vibration. You might not experience directly what you are worried about. A drama could easily occur in an entirely different area of your life and you would have no idea that the energy that created it came from this other situation that you were concerned about. Most people don't look behind the scenes of their lives; consequently, they have no perspective as to how the dots are connected. Then we get to hear the wail, "WHY ME?"

When it comes to manifesting and thoughts, the universe is all inclusive. It doesn't see the word or concept of "not," "no," or "I don't want ..." It only sees where you're putting your energy. When you fight against something, you are putting energy into it, and as a consequence, it expands. When the government says they are conducting a "war on terror," they are actually increasing it. And this has proven to be the case. When we had our war on drugs, drug use actually went up. How about our war on teenage pregnancy?

Mother Theresa, when asked to participate in anti-war rallies and demonstrations, always declined. But she also made the point of adding that any time they would have a rally for peace she would gladly be there.

You name it; whatever you're focused on expands. So don't you think it would be beneficial to actually focus on what you want to occur and literally become that energy for as little as seventeen seconds? Within the science of understanding group consciousness, experiments have been conducted around the globe for decades. Thousands of trained meditators around the world would enter a state of peacefulness at certain times of the day. Each experiment would last a certain period of time with violence worldwide being measured. The results have consistently shown amazing drops in all forms of violence during those times. They were focused on BEING peace. These individuals weren't praying for peace, which carries with it the focus of not having peace. This is the problem with prayer in the manner many people use it. They were simply focused on creating the beingness of peace within themselves and holding it for as long as they could. As such, this was the energy that was radiating out into the cosmos and when you have thousands combining their energies consciously the effects can be amazing. You see, we are the true instruments of peace, not some outside agency.

You want your child to be safe and secure. I get that. So maintain an awareness of what they are doing, especially when they are little. When you are aware, you are fully present in the moment. You aren't projecting into the future. Young children are going to explore their world. It is what they do and yes, from time to time you are going to have to redirect them away from something that might be dangerous, but that is very different from worrying.

As the kids get older our worries move from the arena of just keeping them safe to what choices they are making. Humanity has had fears of making a wrong choice since we first moved from the non-physical realms and into physicality. There was a lot of trauma associated with this initial movement; as a consequence, our trust on many levels was damaged. It is our lack of self-trust that manifests itself in our pattern of finding fault with one choice over another.

This incessant desire to find fault with our choices has also led us into finding fault not only with ourselves but with every individual around us. These patterns have been carried in our cellular memory for eons as we have worked to heal them. Finally, the Quantum children are coming into this world where their consciousness has healed to the extent that these patterns are no longer showing up. They can, however, be conditioned by you, so what are you modeling for them?

Every time you find fault outside yourself you are also finding fault within. In order for Separation consciousness to perpetuate itself, it must keep you in a constant state of seeking. All forms of comparison are an aspect of this function. Look at the subtleties in your daily life, at how many different ways you judge and compare two or more different things. What I am asking of you is to start awakening your ability to choose without judgment. In the next chapter, I will be sharing some tools with you on how to do just that.

Worrying is Actually Part
of our Fight or Flight System

There have been many studies over the years on worry. One such study revealed that:

- 40% of what people worry about never happens
- 30% of worries are in the past and cannot be changed
- 12% are groundless worries about health
- 10% are petty worries about unimportant matters
- Of the remaining 8%, half are things over which we have no control
- That leaves just 4%

Worrying is actually part of our fight/flight system where we are constantly on watch, looking out for danger. It is part of our system that is on such a high alert level you'd think we could be dealing with a saber-toothed tiger at any minute. But let's face it, ninty nine point nine percent of our lives don't need this level of watchfulness. When you look at a worry or a concern, one way to take the energy out of it is to really consider the probability of its outcome. Normally, you'll find that the probability of the unwanted outcome occurring is really extremely small. The brain, however, loves to create a loop around the fear and can play it over and over regardless of the likelihood of the occurrence. One technique you could use to quiet the mind is to only worry to the same degree that the event is plausible. This will get you moving in the right direction while you learn to quiet your mind.

The Pygmalion Effect

Another problem with worry comes from how you see your son or daughter. The best thing you can always do is to see your children in their highest light. In so doing, this is the energy you'll be sending to them. It merges and blends with their energy to the extent that your child is ready to accept it. For some, your energy as a parent may be absorbed and integrated into the child's energy right away.

For others, it may take years before it is accepted. It is all up to the individual. In essence, we are setting the energy aside for them to pick up when they are ready. Ideally, you could see them as amazing divine creators, present in the moment and following their hearts. Their life path flowing before them effortlessly. Sounds pretty good, doesn't it? However, the reality of how we look at them is quite different. Due to our familiarity with them, we know their strengths and their weaknesses, and all too often we focus on the latter.

The term "Pygmalion effect" comes from an ancient Greek story about an amazing sculptor. Pygmalion was a talented artist who could sit with a piece of stone and see within it the exact shape and form it desired to be. In one particular piece of marble, he saw a shape of such beauty that it took his breath away. A woman — but not just any woman. What he saw represented to him the highest potential of all that was female. When he finished sculpting the statue he named her Galatia. He couldn't help but fall in love with her. Of course, Pygmalion was not in love with the statue; he was in love with the idyllic energy that he had seen in it. To him, that energy was real. He beseeched Aphrodite, the Goddess of Love, to bring the statue to life, and seeing that his heart was true, she granted his request.

The Pygmalion effect, as psychologists like to call it, is true and measurable. It is a demonstration of how one person's beliefs can have a beneficial or negative effect on others. In 1968 Dr. Robert Rosenthal and Leonore Jacobson, an elementary school principal in San Francisco, conducted a groundbreaking experiment at her school. They had all the students take a standardized test and then told the teachers which students the test had identified as individuals that would perform exceptionally that year. Unbeknownst to the teachers, the names of those that would be the high performers that year were chosen completely at random. The teachers were also instructed not to give any special treatment or additional attention to those students, and that they would be monitored throughout the year. It is important to note that the children were never told anything. Sure enough, at the end of the year, in every classroom, those students who had been identified to their teachers did, in fact, outperform the rest of the group.

Dr. Rosenthal's subsequent analysis observed small, subtle ways in which the teachers interacted with their students. One of the most interesting things was how a teacher would react to an incorrect answer. If a student was not thought of very highly by the teacher, the teacher might simply accept an incorrect response and move on. If, however, the teacher expected more, she would probe for a deeper answer from the student. This is an example of what was observed from a physical perspective, but we also know that thoughts create and as a consequence there is energy moving behind the scenes that a psychologist cannot see. What is actually occurring is a type of group consciousness effect. The teacher's energy and expectations are being combined in a positive nature with that of her students.

The Pygmalion effect has been demonstrated in many different fields. The business field was very interested in it and, sure enough, psychologists found that teams performed much better when their leader saw them in a very positive light versus the teams whose leaders saw their particular group in a negative one.

You can imagine how this effect might play out in schools and many areas of life when children are labeled in a particular way. Having a remedial class in school is a perfect way to create a low self-fulfilling prophesy.

What do you think happens energetically in a medical situation when your doctor sees your condition as incurable? Is he helping or hurting? Most people who do not understand the Pygmalion effect would think that if he didn't tell you, there wouldn't be any effect: that his thoughts and beliefs are separate from the patient's. But the different experiments in this area have proven otherwise. Normally, doctors will tell you something — and certainly some are more tactful than others. But what do you think happens behind the scenes energetically when you add your worries to theirs? If you accept their opinions, your brain will start to form a story around the situation and the more you focus on it, the more you begin to own it. At this point in time, you'll be literally affirming to the universe that you have that condition — and the more it becomes a part of your story the harder it is to heal.

The Genius Within Each of Us

Your thoughts as a parent do matter a lot. Your child came into this world bringing specific gifts and talents that he or she wishes to express. With your help, hopefully, they will live their passion. Each of us has genius within, and it is our job as a collective to express our gifts and help those around us do the same. The Pygmalion effect demonstrates that you don't have to know what your son or daughter's genius is in order to benefit them. Knowing that they have gifts to express is sufficient enough and the same goes for yourself. How and when those gifts will express themselves, however, is unique to each individual.

I would love to have each and every one of us see our children as geniuses. It would be amazing to see society's transformation. Of course, before this occurs we would have to see ourselves as geniuses first. Can you imagine how you would feel about yourself if you truly knew at your core that you were a genius? Pretty awesome, isn't it? We can't just think about ourselves or our children as geniuses. We have to KNOW it. We have to BELIEVE it. For this to happen, our perspective has to change. Most people, if you were to ask them, would only look at academic intelligence as a determinant of genius. How limiting is that?! We are so much more, but unless you change your perspective and own the fact that genius can be expressed in an infinite number of ways, then you most likely will allow society to condition you into believing that you are less than.

Within all the possibilities of seeing someone in their highest light, many of the thoughts you'd normally have would be centered on their talents and passions. But let me go back to the phrase that I mentioned earlier and expand on its benefits as well.

Seeing yourself, your daughter, your son, your spouse, as well as all those around you as:

Divine creator beings;
present in the moment;
living life through their heart

Allow me to explain where this comes from and what it does for those around you.

Creator being

Each and every person on our planet is a **creator being,** whether they realize it or not. When you own this perspective for yourself and model it for your children, you begin to dissolve completely the energy of victimhood. You stop worrying as a parent because your child will have learned to own and take responsibility for his experiences. When this occurs, it becomes easier to embrace our successes as well as our challenges equally. I like to work from the point of view that if I created it, then there has to be a gift within my creation. Is there something I can learn or grow from by my participation in this experience? Finding the gift can sometimes be a challenge but that doesn't mean it doesn't exist. I can, however, guarantee one thing for you: the more you look, the more you'll find you have eyes to see.

For years, I have asked my kids about their experiences. Their perspective on the situation is far more important than mine because the truest answers lie within them and not me. My asking their opinion models the fact that I see everything they are creating in their lives has value, and I'm constantly reminding them to look within for the answers.

Divine creator being

This is probably the one aspect in our lives that people have more blocks on than any other. People in our society have been conditioned for thousands of years to see themselves as less than and this conditioning is not easily unraveled overnight. Say to yourself,

"...I am a creator of my reality," and feel how it moves through your body. Did it flow and feel light or did it get stuck somewhere? Now try it with "...I am a Divine creator being" and see what you get. Don't worry; you aren't alone if that second saying stuck pretty quickly within your body. And yet...

In order to see the divinity in others,
you must first be able to see it within yourself.
For those with eyes to see.

The simplest place to start owning your Divinity is to recognize that Source energy flows through all things, and as souls we are fully connected to Source. Another way of looking at it is that we are each an aspect of Source that is having a human experience. As such, we are each one hundred percent human but we are also one hundred percent divine at the same time. Now, this doesn't mean that we are operating from our divinity. I wish we were, but it is pretty obvious that most of the world is still operating from its fears, its wounds and its egos. As we each heal our wounds and disconnect from the illusion of our fears, the truth of who we are will show itself more and more. We are living in a timeframe of great transparency where all our internal illusions and veils are disappearing. As you can imagine, the more this occurs the more our true selves begin to show themselves. It doesn't matter if you are Mother Theresa, Jesus, Mother Mary or the worst of us. You are still an aspect of Source having a human experience.

Each of us is growing through our own personal life lessons and you are where you are. You are going through the process of reawakening your authentic self, and recognizing your creatorship and connection to Source. Owning this energy and making your choices from it is a life lesson that each of us is playing out in our own individual way.

Present in the moment

Needless to say, people don't have nearly the same number of blocks in this area as they do around owning their Divinity, but this area can cause just as many problems. So much of what we do is habitual, run by subconscious patterns. As a consequence, we aren't paying attention to where our minds are. And yet all of our creations come from the NOW.

Your children and your spouse know when you are present with them and when you are off somewhere else. Anything you do to improve your focus will always be of benefit to you in everything you do. Meditation and learning how to quiet the mind is certainly a wonderful place to start.

Over the last forty years, individuals have been arriving on this planet with the ability to process enormous amounts of information. Their minds move in ways that my generation never thought even possible. If you have ever watched one of the kids today play a video game, you get a pretty good idea that these children can focus when they want to. We need to do a better job of being creative if we are going to keep their interest. Still, any activity that they can engage in to help their focus and to be present in the moment is going to be of benefit.

Living life through your heart

I believe this thought can be expressed in a number of ways. Pick whichever you might like the most.

- Living life through your heart
- Follow your heart
- Live your passion
- Listen to your heart
- Follow your soul's path

All these are about living your life's purpose. Sir Ken Robinson calls it "finding your element." Ken has written three excellent books on the subject and I highly recommend them.

For thousands of years, we have had the saying, "follow your heart." The reason is simple; this is where we receive our soul-level guidance. Yet, think about how many times we've asked someone what they were thinking when they made a particular choice. Scientific thinking has conditioned us to believe that the mind is where the answer lies. As a consequence, many people have disconnected their hearts from their minds. The reconnection of these two is vital for each and every one of us as we move forward. The mind was designed to implement the soul's choices. It was never meant to be in control, the heart was.

Behind the Scenes

Your energy as a parent is constantly interacting with that of your son's or daughter's. There is no separation. You are constantly modeling for your child. If you are creating experiences based on fear, lack or limitation in your life then that is exactly what is being absorbed energetically by your child. If you are the living embodiment of happiness, then that is the example that your child is going to see and absorb, day in and day out. How each child integrates the energy is always up to the individual, but it certainly doesn't take a research scientist to determine that the positive aspect is going to give your child a big boost in living a happy and healthy life. Can you imagine the kind of example you can set for your children when you are living through your passions and joy?

Our connection and effect on our children happen long before they are born. It begins with the making of a soul contract and the state of consciousness at the time of conception. The reason I mention the soul contract first is that it could come long before the conception of the child. Often, the incoming soul will work with our energy long before he or she ever becomes a gleam in daddy's eye. However, that isn't always the case. Technically, soul contracts could be formed any time during the pregnancy. And then we have the pregnancy itself. How much love you feel for yourself, as well as each other, creates a vibration throughout the body that is vital for the Quantum children. Everything that is going on with the mother and father during the pregnancy is absorbed by the growing fetus.

An incoming soul already knows everything about you: your strengths, your weaknesses, and most importantly your soul's path. This is available to them long before conception. The soul even has the capability to adjust the DNA and genes of its forming fetus in the mother's womb. The incoming soul is capable of working in all areas of the pregnancy. Believe it or not, it could even change the gender of the child up to about the seventh month if it really wanted or needed to. The intriguing thing with this is that the mother normally will not feel or sense any of the changes. (Michaels, 2014)

The child chooses you, the parent, based on all the potentials available that you can provide. Everything is taken into account. Your health, level of joy and happiness that you create around you, your economic status and education, and all other aspects of life that are potentially available through you as a parent. But the pregnancy period is very dynamic and things can change. Eventually, the soul's path is constructed with advice from many different levels of consciousness. Many of you have heard about spirit guides and Guardian Angels, but this is only a small aspect of the aid that is given to us from the spirit side.

Ultimately, a choice is made and a soul contract is formed between the incoming soul and its parents and grandparents. One of the misconceptions that society has is that the soul enters the body immediately upon conception. The soul as an infinite being can enter into the body at any point in time, even several days after birth. I know it sounds strange, but this is how it was explained to me. So, one way or another, at some point in time the soul begins to enter the body. This is never done all at once. There is a gradual introduction that occurs, like a testing of the link or connection prior to turning on or booting up a system. Sometimes changes occur mid-pregnancy. A different soul could be chosen to come in versus the previous one. Another change that could happen has to do with timing. It is possible for a miscarriage to occur if the soul determines that a later time might be better. Of course, there are also physical problems that could cause a miscarriage, but it is just as common that there may be an influence from the other side of the veil. All things are possible.

As the mother moves through her pregnancy, the cells of the growing fetus are formed from the cells of the mother's body. Everything that is going on with the mother on every level is passed on through the cells. Remember, everything is energy. Every form of energy that is affecting the mother is also affecting the child simultaneously. That energy is absorbed and imprinted within the cells of the growing fetus. Interestingly, one of the greatest gifts that the mother provides to the baby is her own personal self-image. Many of you may think back and consider this as both a gift and a curse. When we recognize that there are many types of soul-level lessons we're working within our own self-mastery, it is easier to accept that these influences are a gift and consequently there is no victimhood. Everything that you are, how you feel about yourself, how you feel about life, your connection to Source, everything is coded into the cells that go about forming the body that will be home to your soul during its physical experience.

Early Years and Mirror Neurons

During their early years, children constantly absorb information about their environment. It is a natural instinct that we all have as part of our learning process. Up until the age of seven, everything going on around them is absorbed and recorded at the subconscious level of the brain. Our analytical brain with its filters doesn't come into play until around the age of seven or eight. During our formative years, patterns are constantly being created within our brains regarding how to survive in this new world that we have entered, and the primary source of these patterns comes from our parents.

With the advent of the EEG (electroencephalograph), psychologists found that children's brains stayed primarily in the brainwave states of Alpha and Theta. The cognitive state of "Beta" does not begin to show itself until around age seven. Alpha and

Theta are our relaxed brain states that enable us to do our greatest learning. They are also the states that I work with as a hypnotherapist. This is our gateway to our subconscious and unconscious. If you were to realize that your child is recording everything you do, everything you say, and how you react to your environment, would you go through life in the same way or would you attempt to be a better model?

As I mentioned earlier, Dr. Giacomo Rizzolatti and his team in Italy discovered a type of neuron in the brain that he referred to as a "mirror neuron." These neurons fire in response to seeing a particular behavior. Later, when the subject demonstrated the behavior, the same neurons fired, hence the name "mirror neurons." And these weren't just physical movements that were being mirrored. Emotions were found to be mirrored as well. Every time neurons fire in sequence within the brain they begin to form patterns. The more frequently these patterns are used, the wider and stronger the connections become.

Your energy and your states of consciousness are constantly interacting with everything around you, but due to our illusions of separation, we aren't aware of all that we are affecting. If I do something directly to someone, it would have an effect. But there is so much more going on behind the scenes that the average person is not aware of. As we mirror other peoples' behaviors, activities or languages, we create a group consciousness between two, five, seven, and sometimes even more. However, because of Separation consciousness, the natural tendency is to see yourself as a parent, well, separate.

Points to Remember

1. Worrying is actually a fear of a possible future outcome that we project toward our children. We are putting our energy into exactly what we don't want to have happen.

2. When it comes to manifesting and thoughts, the universe is all inclusive. It doesn't see the word or concepts of "not," "no," or "I don't want ..." It only sees where you're putting your energy.

3. Ideally, you could see your children as amazing divine creators, present in the moment and following their hearts. Their life path flowing before them effortlessly. (The Pygmalion Effect)

4. Do you **know** in your heart that your child has genius within them or do you just **think** it?

5. You are one hundred percent human **and** one hundred percent divine.

6. Our connection and effect on our children happens long before they are born.

7. The child chooses you, the parent, based on all the potentials available that you can provide.

Section 3
Healthy and Happy

7

Healthy and Happy

Doesn't "healthy and happy" sum up what every parent wants for their children?

I guarantee that if you polled any number of parents, "happy and healthy" would show up high on their list.

You as a parent or grandparent are constantly modeling. If you want to teach your child to be happy, become the embodiment of happy. How deeply do you laugh? How much joy do you find in the little moments of life? It is easy to get wrapped up in the day-to-day aspects of life. A mother with young children is probably the busiest person on the planet. There is always something to do, but how long does it take to offer a smile to those around you — or even more importantly — to yourself?

The problem with most of society is it has been working from a backward assumption. That is, "I'll be happy when..." As I've already mentioned, the universe doesn't act in this manner. Thinking you will become happy after a set of circumstances occurs is an empty promise that we have played with throughout the years. You might feel happy for a short period of time but that feeling fades quickly. As soon as you think you have reached that elusive goal, your mind can just as quickly move it out of reach again.

Life was meant to be lived through the energy of Joy; anything other than this has been conditioned by humanity and doesn't have to be as such. When we take on the perspective of Joy and Happiness **first**, the rest of the universe aligns to our perspective. Each of us came to this experience with a purpose. Aligning with our purpose, finding our Element, living our passions, following our fascinations, and being in service is where we normally find our greatest Joy. We live life through our senses and find pleasure in them, but don't confuse pleasure with Joy. Joy comes from your heart and soul.

Positive psychologists such as Sean Achor have spent years studying the positive effects of being happy first. It makes our bodies healthier. Our brains work better. Our ability to solve problems is enhanced. We get better results in virtually any task that one designs. And yet most people still believe the events of their lives should define how they should feel. This is the victim persona that we have played with as a consciousness for millenniums. We are constantly choosing a particular perspective through which to view our reality. And that choice leads to how we feel in any given moment.

One of my favorite portions I read about in Sean's book, *The Happiness Advantage*, was where the researchers wanted to see if they could change the atmosphere and culture in a hospital using a technique called the five/ten approach. This technique was employed at a very high-end hotel, and the psychologists wanted to see if it could be implemented in a hospital and what changes could be observed. Any time an employee was with ten feet of a guest, they were to smile. When they were within five feet, they were to say something pleasant such as, "Hello" or "Are you having a good day?" Then you would allow the mirror neurons to go to work. I see something similar when I enter the lobby at the bank where the tellers are taught to greet their clients by name. Obviously, this technique is designed to create a friendly, comfortable atmosphere.

As you can imagine, the staff at the hospital that was used to working with the patients in a very close manner had no problem implementing the five/ten approach. The doctors, however, had a much more difficult time. They are taught from the beginning of med school to disconnect from their patients; to be completely clinical. Despite their years of conditioning, even they finally succumbed to the power of the mirror neurons. After a year, statistics indicated that patient satisfaction and likelihood to refer others to their facility had gone up significantly. Things can change when you change your perspective.

Tuning In

Years ago I was given a saying by Jeshua and Mary Magdalene that I was to use as both mantra and affirmation. Interestingly, the angelic realm treats this phrase as a prayer. Allow me to share it with you:

"I choose the path of Joy"

To me the emphasis of "I choose…" cannot be overstated. I am not hoping for Joy. I am making an active choice to live joyfully and the universe is responding in kind. Here is one way you can play with this mantra.

❖ When you have a choice, start first by feeling the energy of "I choose the path of Joy." Sit with it for a moment. Really play with how that feels for you.

❖ Next, feel the energy of the choices that are before you.

❖ Which choice resonates with the feeling you felt within your body when you made the affirmation?

❖ Simply play a matching game with the choices that are before you and in doing so you'll be choosing without giving the other choices any energy.

Some of you may remember the old TV show "Concentration" where the contestants attempted to match squares on a game board. Each contestant would have the host of the show turn over two squares that they thought were the same. In a similar fashion, you are simply matching your choices to the vibration of "the path of Joy." If a particular choice does not feel the same as the vibration of Joy, simply go on to the next possibility. There is no need for judgment. Say the affirmation to yourself over and over throughout your day, and you will see how easy it is to know within you when a choice is a match. From this position there is no "less than" or "greater than" or "better than." You are simply making choices that resonate with Joy. And let's face it…if it's not about Joy, why are you doing it?

115

Another version of this is to feel whether a belief or choice is "**light**" or "**heavy**" within your body. If something feels light within us, it normally is aligned with the truth of who we are. So as you go about your day, constantly feel the choices before you. Your body is constantly talking to you. The information is subtle and in order to hear it, you must learn how to quiet all the chatter. In essence, this is the beginning of you becoming a body whisperer. This is one of the easiest techniques that can be taught to young children.

My entire family, my wife and three kids all started working with energy by studying Reiki back in the 90s. Even my youngest daughter, Katie, who was born in 1988, participated. Over the years, I have studied many different healing-hands modalities, as well as how to get information from the body. Learning how to use a **pendulum** was a natural extension of these studies. A pendulum is a great beginning tool for children because they can see the energy move. Both my daughters had no problem picking up the techniques, young as they were. We practiced with every kind of question you could imagine. What to have for lunch, which way should we drive to school? You name it: we would ask using the pendulum. Was this overkill? Of course, but you want to practice with questions that have minor consequences as a beginner before you move up to more important questions. One of the things that I found fascinating was how my personal biases would come into my answers. If I was asking a question and was very neutral about it, my answers were normally correct. So, if I knew that I had a bias in regard to a particular question/answer, I would have someone else that was neutral to the choice ask the pendulum for me.

In training my daughter, I told her that I would support her in any action as long as she could show me that it was in "her best and highest interest." In doing so she was trained for independence from a very young age. When your children's choices are in alignment with their best and highest interest, all we need to do as parents is sit back and enjoy their journey. All forms of control are released, and we truly can trust and allow them their path.

Tapping into your heart/soul information has to be one of the most important paths to Joy and happiness that we can ever choose. There are many different techniques available to you. I am only offering a few. Your job is to find the ones that work for you and master them.

For many of you, this could be the first time you have attempted to feel your soul's information coming through your body instead of just turning the question over in your mind. So be patient with yourself.

Appendix 5 has a whole set of references on kinesiology (muscle testing) that you can view on YouTube. It is always easier to learn a technique if you can see it in action.

*****

The art of the question is important in these techniques. How we phrase a question is vital to the information we receive. A poorly phrased question is not going to help you in any way. It is very easy to be misled and confused instead of enlightened. Let's play with an example that is simple, like deciding whether or not it is beneficial to eat an apple.

1. *Is it in my best and highest interest to eat this apple?*
2. *Is it in my best and highest interest to eat this apple at this time?*
3. *Is consuming an apple in my body's best and highest interest?*
4. *Should I eat an apple?*
5. *Does my body want an apple at this time?*

Do you see how examples 1 and 2 are both pretty good, but example 2 is a little bit more specific because of the addition of a timeframe?

Do you see how example 3 is open-ended and brings in the possibility that there might be sometime in the future where eating an apple might be a problem? Who knows, you might be sick or whatever.

Example 4 is where you aren't making a choice. It is like you want something other than yourself to make a choice for you. What we are attempting to do with our various questions is to determine if something is in alignment with our truth, and from that perspective, we make a choice.

Example 5 opens us to two interesting concepts that you need to consider. First, I am not my body. I am a human soul having a physical experience and the vessel that is housing my soul is my body. The other concept is that we live in a sea of energy and that we are constantly picking up thoughts from other people. In fact, ninety eight percent of your thoughts and feelings originate with other people. Taking a moment to determine if something is yours or not is always going to be extremely useful. Which brings us to two follow-up questions.

> *Is this thought mine?*
> *Is this thought someone else's?*

If you get a yes to these questions, simply return the energy to them and start over.

There are many different questions you can play with over time but one that I've found extremely fascinating once again comes from Dain Heer.

How can it get any better than this?

This little question can be used in many positive ways. Any time the events of your day go a little south, instead of dwelling on them, shift to, "How can it get any better than this?" When you do, you open yourself up to the positive. So in general everything becomes "this or better." This question is asked both within and to the universe. It most specifically is **not** asked to the analytical mind. We are creating a point of view that magic can happen at any time, anywhere and then allowing it to occur. So many of us block the "allowing." This fun little question is amazing at helping us get out of our own way.

118

We are going to look at different beliefs on health and I want you to have some tools to play with so that you can feel for yourself what is true for you. It is important to understand that because something might feel right for you does not mean that it has to be true for someone else. If you are asking a question that concerns one of your children, recognize that your biases can come into play and be aware. Your job is to keep asking questions and to continue to practice. It is the only way to grow skills in this area.

Trust

One of the fascinating things about tuning within for answers is the level of healing that occurs in the process. Many of you might think the answer to your question would be more important but that is not necessarily true. What are being healed are aspects of your **trust of yourself** and **trust of your soul**.

Our internal loss of trust was our first and greatest loss as we initially moved into the physical plane and began taking on carbon-based forms. Now as we move along the ascension spiral, the last vestiges of our original wounds are coming to the surface to be addressed.

Each and every time you activate internal communication between your human self and soul self, you express trust in both, by simply offering room for mutual self-expression.

Points to Remember

1. "I'll be happy when..." is backwards to how the universe works.

2. Adopt the five/ten approach.

3. I **choose** the path of Joy.

4. *How can it get any better than this?*

5. When you tune within, you are healing aspects of your **trust of yourself** and **trust of your soul**.

6. Each and every time you activate internal communication between your human self and soul self, you express trust in both, by simply offering room for mutual self-expression.

8

An Interesting Point of View

There are many points of view within the medical community that people are working with, and each individual loves to see his point of view as correct and the other's incorrect. "Black and white," is how we have been trained to look at things. This judgment is extremely harmful because it closes us to possibility. I have my beliefs, a medical doctor has his, and an integrative doctor will have another perspective and so on. What if we were all right and wrong at the same time?

One of the reasons I like some of the tools that Dain Heer and Access Consciousness use is because they address this paradox. What if you simply saw every perspective as just "an interesting point of view?" Do you feel how judgment would lose its energy? There are many points of view that you are going to be exposed to as a parent or grandparent regarding your health and that of your family. Each may be a view that can be of benefit to you. Your job is to be open to all possibility and feel for yourself what feels lighter.

This is especially true for our beliefs around scientific facts. Did you know that there is virtually no area of scientific understanding from one hundred years ago that has not been changed in some fashion? And today's scientific facts are different...how? Let's just call all of them an interesting point of view and then we can include everything just as the universe does.

I have the interesting point of view that everything is energy. As such, it can always be changed and transmuted. From this perspective everything is curable. Does this make you feel lighter or heavier?

The current medical model began to take shape in the early 1900s when investors such as John D. Rockefeller decided to invest heavily in the health sector, specifically pharmaceuticals. Their point of view was that a model based on pharmaceuticals and expensive surgeries would be the most profitable. To individuals such as Rockefeller, "competition was a sin." Seeing medicine as nothing more than a business, they went about the systematic elimination of any modality that they couldn't control or charge for. Profit— not your health— became the number one priority.

In the early 1900s naturopathy, herbal medicine, chiropractic care, acupuncture, homeopathy and allopathic medicine all shared the healthcare pie. Allopathic practices were considered at the time the least desirable of all the modalities. Have you ever heard the term "death by cure?" At that time, you were just as likely to be killed by the modality as by the malady you were dealing with. Currently, the World Health Organization ranks our healthcare in the United States thirty-seventh just ahead of Slovenia and Cuba. Dr. Barbara Starfield of the Johns Hopkins School of Hygiene and Public Health found in her research that traditional medical care was the third leading cause of death in America, ranked behind only cancer and heart disease.

The current model is based on the interesting point of view that sees the physical body like a machine and that a broken part could be isolated and changed without any consequence to the rest of the body. It is based on concepts of Newtonian physics. Natural philosopher and seventeenth century scientist, Sir Isaac Newton developed a set of universal principles to help explain and predict the motion of objects in the natural world. Basically, his theory proposed the entire physical world worked on specific laws like a giant intricate machine. Everything was based on cause and effect that came from precise physical laws.

Today, however, we have both quantum and Newtonian points of view and at any one point in time, each might be correct. If I have a car accident and break my arm, there is a cause and effect on the physical level, but energetically there are other levels that also come

122

into play. I chose at some level to be in my car at that place and time. Why did I choose to participate within this experience? What were the other quantum potentials that were also available within this experience? What was I to learn? What was the gift? Was this possibly an emotional issue that needed clearing?

Another very important perspective that allopathic medicine bases a lot of its assumptions on is from the Germ Theory brought forth by Pasteur in the late 1880s. Did you know there was another equally correct theory which also existed at the same time that wasn't adopted?

When you look at germ theory, what you are looking at is a victim consciousness theory. This theory, as it was put forth by Pasteur, meant that disease is caused by an outside agent, normally a germ. This assumption is based upon the correlation that when a disease occurs a germ is also present. The problem with this is it assumes the germ caused the disease. It's creating a correlation that may or may not be correct.

Modern medicine believes this to be correct and therefore operates from the perspective that if the germs could be eradicated, then the disease would also be exterminated. Hence, we have the one hundred year war where the medical community has fought to save us from some dreaded outside pathogen.

The competing view to this assumption comes from a very highly decorated French scientist named Antoine Bechamp. He believed that a healthy body could be immune to harmful bacteria and that only when cells become weak and ill could bacteria cause a destructive effect. Bechamp continued to discover that healthy tissue was constantly being exposed to bacteria, but only as the body started to deteriorate or weaken would the bacteria change due to the changes in the body's cell biochemistry. His primary point of emphasis was that the environment of the body was key and crucial to our health. If the environment were healthy, dis-ease would not occur. True preventive medicine focuses on this kind of

123

understanding. Alternatively, traditional medicine focuses on killing germs. Unfortunately, this process frequently does as much harm as it does good.

Bechamp's and Pasteur's theories are equally important for a healthy life, but unfortunately, medications for killing bacteria have become a huge industry and it is easier to blame germs rather than being responsible for your diet, your eating habits and your thoughts.

When you understand how thoughts create realities and how our states of being can affect the body, you quickly can understand how Bechamp's point of view is in alignment with quantum understandings. We become empowered when we take responsibility for our own health.

For years, I have looked behind the scenes and tried to determine for myself or others why or how any particular event or set of circumstances had occurred. Not once, in all of that time did I find the answer to be *that the individual involved was a victim*. WE are constantly creating our realities; just because you don't know why doesn't mean that you didn't create it somehow.

As an intuitive working with understandings from the Quantum children, I have been given the interesting viewpoint that their DNA has changed. This would mean that their physical bodies are different and as a consequence many standard practices of the medical community could have unintended results. And certainly this is what we are seeing. The problem is that the business of medicine is refusing to adapt and change because of the money/profit involved.

As we get lighter in our vibration, we become more energy and less mass. Energy medicine has become more effective in its adaptations because it can shift and change in frequency and wavelength more easily. Bruce Lipton, PhD, MD, a cellular biologist from Stanford and the University of Wisconsin has found in his research that the cells of our body are one hundred times more receptive to energy and information than they are to chemical substances such as those found in a pharmaceutical drug.

As I have mentioned before, these new children are more sensitive than previous generations. This is showing itself in numerous areas that will affect their medical care. In one of my meditations the message, "**Watch the Dosage**" overwhelmed me. I've never felt something so powerful coming to me before or since. There are many allopathic medicine practices that are based upon old data from previous generations. Conventional perspective maintains that things don't change and the more data one has the better. But things have changed. The Quantum children may look like any other but under the hood, vibrationally they're quite different.

Standard of Care

Most people believe if a university does a study and proves that something is a useful treatment that doctors can read this study and automatically start using that for their patients. Unfortunately, this is incorrect. In the United States, we have what is called Standard of Care. Each time your physician makes a diagnosis, he or she enters a code into their computer and the FDA's standard of care treatment is activated. So whether you want it or not, this is what you are going to get, or the physician risks losing his or her license. The problem with this is twofold: first, allopathic medicine is constantly operating years if not decades behind, and second, there has been a complete loss of individuality.

Dr. Jerry Tennant, in an interview with Regina Meredith on Gaim TV, offered this example. (Tennant, 2016)

> *One of my friends in Dallas had a heart attack and was in the hospital. The next morning they brought a bunch of pills in and he asked the nurse..."what is that pill for?"*
>
> *Nurse - That is to lower your blood pressure.*
>
> *Man - But my blood pressure is ninety over fifty. If you lower it any more I'll pass out.*

> *Nurse - It doesn't matter. It is the standard of care that anybody that comes into the hospital with your condition has to have blood pressure medicine.*
>
> *Man - Okay, Well what is that other pill for?*
>
> *Nurse - It is to lower your cholesterol.*
>
> *Man - So what is my cholesterol?*
>
> *Nurse - I don't know we haven't measured it.*
>
> *Man - So why do I have to take a cholesterol pill?*
>
> *Nurse - Because it is the standard of care.*

This is not an isolated incidence. I've heard of numerous circumstances similar to this.

Let's say for example that I magically found a cure for X disease. As I said before, I can't just publish it in a journal and have doctors start using my cure. I would have to go to the FDA, and spend millions of dollars over five years or more to get them to give me permission to say that my cure works. Then, the protocol needs to be accepted by different boards of doctors as standard practice and this takes even more time.

So, what we find is that doctors and parents are in a very difficult place. On the one hand, if the doctors don't follow accepted practice and something happens they can be sued. And yet, if they follow accepted practice with all that that entails the chance of causing more harm than good is also there. One of the main parts of a doctor's creed is "to do no harm." Unfortunately, this is not the case anymore and the only person that can step in and say "no" is you. I realize this is a burden you don't wish to carry. You have been conditioned for one hundred years to give your power away to the man or woman wearing the white coat. However, NOW is the time you absolutely must take it back.

One of the biggest problems we have today is the boards setting standard care for the pediatricians have been extremely slow to change any part of their protocols. There has been a tremendous amount of evidence showing problems with a number of vaccines and the overuse of antibiotics, and the medical community has made virtually no changes to their accepted care.

The MMR vaccine is the number-one case in point. This vaccine should have been taken off the market two decades ago. The CDC's study in 2004 found a direct link to this vaccine and its toxicity triggering autism. The timing of the vaccine was crucial in the findings. Children getting the vaccine prior to age three were hundreds of times more likely to become autistic than those children that received the vaccine at a later time. Instead of removing this vaccine and going with the much safer single vaccines, Merck was allowed to stop making the single vaccines because they were competing with the MMR. The study's findings were then buried until the lead scientist on the study came forward as a whistleblower in 2014. The movie/documentary *VAXXED* explains the full story. I consider it a must-see for any parent.

One of the greatest disservices by Congress was to make vaccines mandatory. Vaccines should be voluntary, plain and simple. Taking away an individual's free will on what they can do with and to their body is one of the worst things that can be done in any society. And then you have the removal of liability from Big Pharma. If Big Pharma were held accountable, as they should be, they would have cleaned up their products years ago or been forced to take them off the market. Instead, thousands of children have been harmed.

A groundbreaking drug safety study in Shanghai, China, provides needed information about the frequency of vaccine drug reactions among children. Adverse drug reactions are a serious public health concern and are one of the leading causes of morbidity and mortality worldwide. More than five hundred thousand children are treated every year for adverse drug reactions in US outpatient clinics and emergency rooms. The Shanghai study, based on reported pediatric adverse drug reactions (ADRs), in 2009 found that forty two percent were caused by vaccines, ranging from mild skin rashes to deadly

127

reactions like anaphylaxis and death. Of all the drugs causing adverse reactions among children, vaccines are the most commonly reported. This study is particularly significant because the vast majority of reports came from physicians, pharmacists and other healthcare providers. Less than three percent of the reports were from consumers.

In 1988, the Vaccine Injury Compensation Program was created under the National Childhood Vaccine Injury Act, taking away our ability to sue the drug manufacturers. Vaccine injury claims are awarded or denied by the US Department of Health and Human Services using US Department of Justice attorneys. Currently, seventy five percent of all claims are denied and many take more than ten years to settle. And if you were to settle out of court, the fact that a vaccine was the cause of your claim would not be part of the record. It gets even better. The attorneys for the government will cite the falsified CDC study as evidence that your child's autism wasn't caused by the vaccine.

How can it get any better than this for Big Pharma? They get all the profit with none of the liability and the government not only recommends their products, it makes them mandatory. Part of their argument is that no vaccine will ever be one hundred percent safe. If you only had a few cases per year, it would be one thing, but more than five hundred thousand! Who on earth would consider this an acceptable number other than the drug companies? You deserve to choose what is put in your body or that of your children.

As I said at the beginning of this book, "everything is energy." This view leads us to the next understanding and it is, your "state of being" and "consciousness" determine the terrain of your body, not some outside pathogen. Masters for thousands of years have been demonstrating our ability to transmute different forms of imbalances within our bodies. Their message: "If you raise your vibration above that of the toxicity, there is no effect. In fact, the toxin will change." Still, this does not mean I run out every week and drink Drano just to see where my energy is. The point is, we are the creators of our health and our consciousness is the vanguard of this understanding. Our bodies are constantly reflecting back to us everything that is happening in our energetic field. The question is, are we listening?

Science is finally catching up with this as well. In recent studies, scientists have found that activities such as meditation and yoga actually change the practitioner's brain as well as signaling the body to turn on different genes. Previously, scientists thought genes only did one thing. The study of Epigenetics is telling us a whole different story. What we are finding is that over seventy five percent of our genes can switch on or off based on our states of being. The doctors who were studying the meditators found that they had many more genes switched on associated with health and the immune system than those participants in the study that were the control group.

As I mentioned earlier, germ theory is a form of victim consciousness and every aspect of allopathic medicine stems from this concept. Conventional doctors are not taught how consciousness works with one's health. I wish it was part of their course of study but it's not. The primary reality they work with is that of cause and effect within the physical world only. But we have many fields of energy, not just the dense portion that we refer to as "our body."

The good news is that like the rest of humanity, doctors are waking up. Lissa Rankin, MD, is a perfect example of one such doctor. Her book, "Mind over Medicine" tells her story. She is a classically trained OB/GYN who went through a profound awakening. My wife and I have had the pleasure to work exstensively with Dr. Paul Drouin. He is the founder of "Quantum University" in Hawaii. Dr. Drouin was a family physician for twenty five years in Canada and left this practice to follow a "holistic approach to healing." When you hear the term *integrative doctor*, this is the kind of physician who is being referred to. He, along with a host of other amazing instructors, is training a new breed of healthcare practitioners with understandings in quantum physics, not the limited point of view that most allopathic doctors are trained to have. Integrative physicians, along with informational and energy medicine, are the wave of the future.

We have had integrative doctors before. Homeopaths in the late 1800s and early 1900s went to medical school just like every other doctor. It wasn't until the influence of money and associated agendas that the study of homeopathy was forced out of the medical schools. And yet, here we are again. We have come full cycle. Healthcare practitioners, just like the rest of humanity, are awakening. In many ways, it is only the structure of the medical community that is holding them back.

This structure, as with all structures in society, will either move into a fourth density vibration or it will collapse. This is a very important point to understand. Mother Earth has already moved into her higher vibration and where she goes everything else must follow. It may take a little time but it will occur. Structures such as the medical community have to become flexible and adaptable. Considering the way Big Pharma has its grip on the situation, I don't expect the shift to occur gently.

Questions and Choices

In the meantime, you still have choices to make, so let's play with some questions around vaccines and see what feels true for you. Remember, you are to feel for lightness or heaviness in any particular thought.

- *All vaccines are beneficial to my body.*
- *Is this vaccine beneficial to my body?*
- *Is this vaccine in my best and highest interest?*

What did you feel?

Did you know that there are homeopathic versions of every vaccine that carry the energetic signature of the disease or virus without any of the physical components or toxicity? Interesting, yes? So why aren't those promoted? Pretty simple, really. Follow the money.

Play with these sets of questions and see what feels true for you.

- *My body would benefit from a vaccine if all forms of toxicity were removed from it.*
- *An energetic version of a vaccine would be more accepted by my body than those in traditional practice.*

It is important to keep clearing your conditioning around any of these subjects because so many of our thoughts come from other sources. Also, no matter what you choose, make sure your doctor gives you a list of all the ingredients of any vaccine that you are considering, as well as all the side effects. I think you will be shocked to see what is actually in them. You can also get this information from the internet beforehand.

Keep asking questions!

Antibiotics were considered a breakthrough years ago when they first came on the scene. But what we are now seeing is a consistent weakening of our immune system over the generations. Natasha Campbell-McBride, MD, has an interesting view linking our overuse of antibiotics and other practices to the rampant rise in autism, dyslexia, depression, ADD and ADHD. In her book *GAPS: Gut and Psychology Syndrome*, she describes her path in working to cure her son of autism that was induced by a vaccination. What she found in her research was that since the inception of full-spectrum antibiotics, our immune systems have gotten weaker and weaker. Fully eighty percent of our immune system response comes from the beneficial bacteria that live in our intestinal tract.

The siege of our castle began in earnest back in the 40s. It was during World War II that the medical community began using wide-spectrum antibiotics. Every time these antibiotics are used they destroy not only the toxic microbes that the body is dealing with but also the beneficial flora living in the intestinal tract. It takes the body an extensive period of time to repair itself and to rebuild the flora every time antibiotics have been used.

131

In the 1950s and 60s, breastfeeding fell out of favor and powdered infant baby formula was used extensively instead of mother's milk. We have since found that mother's milk provides a baby with many of its initial antibodies. These antibodies are vital for the newborns as they develop their immune systems.

Also, in the 1960s, women began using birth control pills earlier and earlier. Once again introducing a synthetic product into the intestinal tract harming the flora. Even something as small as an aspirin does damage to the flora. So think of all the prescription medications that have been handed out like candy over the years and you'll get an idea of the stress we have put on our tiny little soldiers over the last four generations.

How this translates to the children is very interesting. You see, a new baby's immune system gets its initial charge of beneficial flora from its mother during the birth process. If her flora is compromised and weakened, then so is the child's. When you compile the effects over several generations, then you get to see the kind of impact we are seeing today. Dr. McBride's point of view is vaccines were designed for healthier immune systems than what our children have today and that no child should be given any type of vaccine unless you test their intestinal flora first. This test is easy and inexpensive, costing around a hundred dollars. Dr. McBride recommends further that **no** vaccines be administered to any child before the age of three.

The Hepatitis B vaccine is a perfect example of the craziness that you as a parent need to be aware of. It is given twelve hours after the birth unless **you refuse it**. Your baby has just gone through a very stressful experience during birth and the medical community feels that it is necessary to give them a vaccine right after that. Hepatitis B is associated with a blood-transmitted disease associated with risky lifestyle choices. It is NOT a children's disease. Instead of testing the parents to see if there is actually a risk, the vaccine is given to every child born at one of the worst possible times, regardless of a risk factor.

*According to the Vaccine Adverse Event Reporting System (VAERS), operated jointly by the CDC and FDA, there were 36,788 **officially** reported adverse reactions to Hepatitis B vaccines between 1992 and 2005. Of these, 14,800 were serious enough to cause hospitalization, life-threatening health events or permanent disabilities.*

And 781 people were reported to have DIED following hepatitis B vaccination. (Mercola, Hepatitis B Vaccine: Refuse This Routine Procedure – Or Expose Your Baby's Brain to Severe Danger.., 2010)

In 1996, The National Vaccine Information Center reported eight hundred seventy two adverse reactions to the Hepatitis B vaccine of children under the age of fourteen. There were forty eight deaths. In all of 1996, there were only two hundred seventy nine total cases of Hepatitis B reported for this same age bracket.

*****

In the area of health, my first and foremost recommendation is that you own it. Your health is yours and you need to take care of it every single day by your level of joy, your states of being and your choices.

133

Points to Remember

1. The current model is based on the point of view that sees the physical body like a machine — Newtonian physics.

2. At any one point in time, both quantum and Newtonian points of view might be correct.

3. Germ theory is victimhood consciousness. The care of the Terrain of the body is based in Quantum understandings.

4. **Watch the Dosage**

5. Dr. McBride's point of view is that vaccines were designed for healthier immune systems than what our children have today, and that no child should be given any type of vaccine unless you test their intestinal flora first.

6. Dr. McBride also recommends that no vaccines should be administered before the age of three.

9

Synthetics and Antibiotics

In many ways, it is easy to point one's finger at the obvious problems that allopathic medicine is going through. But those of us that look at the whole health picture see synthetics and antibiotics to be as much of a problem as vaccines and GMOs. This is because they are accepted and used regularly. So any discussion on health has to include some understandings in this area.

Currently, there are more than eighty thousand chemicals that the FDA considers legal that we are exposed to all the time. Most of these are unregulated and have never been studied for their safety. We have, of course, all the pharmaceutical products but this is only part of the story. We also have processed foods, food coloring, cosmetics, and all the chemicals that are put in our drinking water. Most people recognize the need to filter the chlorine and fluoride out of their water, but now I understand that some municipalities are even adding ammonia into their water supply. Seriously!

Dr. Bill Nelson, the inventor of the biofeedback device known as the SCIO and the EDUCTOR, has this story about his first introduction to pharmaceuticals in medical school.

> *My first professor of pharmacology started the course with an announcement. He stood up and said in a deep serious voice,* **"To use a Synthetic anything is an insult to the body."** *He clarified this by explaining that the human body knows when it is given a synthetic. The body naturally can recognize a synthetic and it is an insult. It is not the same; it is similar but not as good or as complete as the natural compounds. Whether it is a vitamin, hormone, enzyme or anything synthetic, it is an insult to the body.*

135

"Now," he explained, "We will spend the rest of this course learning how to Insult the Body." For SINthetics is what modern medicine makes money on.

What Dr. Nelson and his professor are saying is that our bodies don't recognize synthetics as something they're supposed to be using. The body has to be tricked in some fashion. Synthetics carry a different vibration than a product that is natural. In many cases, our bodies react to them, not as something that is beneficial, but as a toxin. The Quantum children are especially sensitive to these.

Think of it this way: the Earth and the new children have evolved and are vibrating at a new frequency and consciousness. Organic produce receiving their energy directly from the sun and Mother Earth will naturally carry the new vibrations as well. All of us are moving our energy to be in alignment with our host planet, and the food and other products that we take into our bodies are either helping or hurting us in this process. Our bodies are able to see, recognize, and assimilate the nutrients and other aspects that these foods might provide. The vibration of a synthetic product, however, is different. Yes, our bodies are able to cope with synthetics for a certain period of time, but as with any toxin, exposure over time takes its toll and problems begin to develop. Normally our reactions aren't instantaneous; consequently, it is hard for us to connect the dots back to the true origin, and this is exactly what the corporations are banking on.

Some corporations create products synthetically, not because they are healthy for you or because it is the only way that you might be able to receive a particular healing element. No, they do it because the law allows them to patent these formulas and therefore control them.

Genetically Modified Organisms or GMOs fall into this category.

From GMO Awareness

Genetic modification is the process of forcing genes from one species into another *entirely unrelated* species.

136

Unlike cross-breeding or hybridization—both of which involve two related species and have been done without ill effects for centuries—genetic engineering forcefully breaches the naturally occurring barriers between species.

Roundup Ready Corn, produced by Monsanto for example, is the combination of Corn + DNA from soil bacteria that is immune to Roundup herbicide + E. coli bacteria + soil bacteria that causes tumors in plants (which enables the plant's cell wall to be breached).

Other examples of GMOs include strawberries and tomatoes injected with *fish genes* to protect the fruit from freezing; goats injected with *spider genes* to produce milk with proteins stronger than Kevlar for use in industrial products; salmon that are genetically engineered with a *growth hormone* that allows them to keep growing larger. The list goes on and on.

GMO crops are now banned in thirty eight countries worldwide. So, any conditioning that tells you most of the world is accepting these products is a complete fabrication. It is important you find out what is in your food, and GMO labeling is a central part of this. The manufacturers of these products spend millions of dollars every year to block this from occurring. We need transparency and the only way we are going to get it is if we demand it.

We will talk more about food and nutrition in the next book, but an important point needs to be made here. You cannot fool your body. It knows what is good for it and what is not. Years ago there was a great deal of focus on our soils and how depleted of mineral content they were. It was described at the time that vegetables such as tomatoes had a fraction of the nutritional value of those grown back in 1900. Then we had the introduction of all the processed foods. Technically, we have been processing food in different ways for thousands of years, but since World War II the food industry began to really increase what it was doing in this area. The box of cardboard that different products were coming in was said to have more nutrition than what was in the box. Because I have been talking about everything being energy, I would like to offer you a different way of looking at food and this would be to consider its life force or vibrancy.

Our bodies are energy-converting machines. When we eat a salad, for instance, we are consuming light that was converted by the plants through photosynthesis. How much light or energy any one fruit or vegetable has varies. The food industry uses all kinds of dyes and preservatives to deceive the eye. Add in the fact that we have been conditioned to believe that bigger is better when frequently a smaller, fresher, piece of fruit will almost always have a higher level of vibrancy than one which has been modified in some fashion just to produce a little bigger product.

Water as well has vibrancy and sure enough, the more it is processed the more it loses its life force. We are trained to believe that the only thing important about water is that it is clean. However, different types of clean water can be just as devoid of energy as the processed foods. Think about it and keep it in mind the next time you make your food and water selections.

Antibiotics and your Intestinal Flora

My wife, Allyn has a PhD in Natural Medicine and we take probiotics every day. We eat organic fruits and vegetables, locally grown when they are in season. Any meat that we eat is range-fed, hormone- and antibiotic-free. Also, we like to do an intestinal cleanse at least once a year. On a physical level, taking care of our intestinal tracts is easily one of our top priorities. It is estimated that eighty percent of our immune system resides within each of our intestinal tracts.

On the surface, we look like we are a single individual but in reality, we are a walking ecosystem. We are the host to trillions of microbes that are absolutely mandatory for our health and most of these reside in our intestinal tract. We know scientifically that compromising this delicate ecosystem can have long- term and even permanent ramifications to our health, and yet many of the standard practices of allopathic medicine harm and sometimes destroy this very sensitive ecosystem. When my wife and I think of preventive medicine, we don't think about early testing and frequent checkups, which is the current practice of conventional medicine. No, we focus on maintaining the health of this vital and fragile community. We look at every practice that we do and how it affects the balance and health of the flora in our digestive system. An individual's diet, medical and dental practices all come into play here.

We currently have setting up residence within our intestines about three to four pounds of these little guys or about one hundred trillion microbes. The friendly bacteria are Probiotic (for-life). The bad bacteria are Antibiotic (against-life). And then you have the viruses which outnumber the bacteria ten to one.

There are great articles on both Dr. Mercola's website (www.mercola.com) as well as Natural News (www.naturalnews.com) that delve into this subject more deeply than I wish to at this point in time. Because of this, I'll keep my comments to a more general nature.

Probiotics benefit us in so many different ways. As I've already mentioned, they are a major part of our immune system. They manufacture certain B vitamins as well as the milk-digesting enzyme lactase. They also produce antibacterial substances that kill or deactivate the non-beneficial bacteria. Probiotics also have an anti-carcinogenic effect since they are active against certain tumors as well. And of course, they are a major part of the efficiency of our digestive tract. But this is just a tip of the iceberg. There is still an awful lot that we don't know.

In general, I believe it would be safe to say that if you have a healthy gut you are well on your way to having a healthy body. This is the foundation upon which our health is built. However, when your gut isn't healthy, everything else you might be doing is most likely to be compromised. So what do we do to affect it, both from a beneficial standpoint and a detrimental one?

The type of diet you eat is a major influence on bacterial health. The bacteria are healthy on a diet rich in complex carbohydrates (vegetables, whole grains, legumes) and low in animal fats, fatty meats, sugars and commercially cultured dairy products. (Experiments have found that common food additives like sodium benzoate and potassium sorbate kill good bacteria.) Not surprisingly, the diet which is best for people is also ideal for healthy bacteria.

There are three standard practices from the medical and dental communities that harm this foundation of our immune system. These are antibiotics, vaccines and silver amalgam dental fillings. These are the big three, but they certainly aren't the only ones. Steroids and hormonal drugs such as cortisone and birth control pills, as well as exposure to other chemicals like chlorine and fluoride in tap water, can cause great damage to the bowel flora.

Certainly the elephant in the room has to be antibiotics. They were hailed as the last century's modern miracle. In essence, they were the super soldiers we now had to combat germs. They were the ultimate answer to Pasteur's germ theory. And now what we are finding is that antibiotics are probably more dangerous to our health than even GMOs — and that says a lot.

So, what exactly do antibiotics do? They kill bacteria. Good or bad, it doesn't matter; they take all bacteria out. Certainly over the years, antibiotics have saved a lot of lives but now we are finding that their overuse is causing more problems than they are preventing. We are exposed to antibiotics in a lot of our food sources, not just from the medical community. As a consequence, some of us may actually be consuming them on a daily basis. The cumulative effect of the exposures can be devastating to our bodies.

Vaccines have been known to contain mercury, formaldehyde and aluminum. Silver amalgam dental fillings contain mercury and are considered a hazardous material. All these products are very damaging to the flora in our digestive system, not to mention their destructive effect on the brain. Dental fillings can even leach their mercury into your system gradually over a twenty year period. These effects compound over time.

There are definitely going to be times when your child is going to benefit from being on antibiotics and other times when they won't. I certainly can't tell you when that might be. You need to tune into and see what feels right for you and your family. Talk to your doctor or pediatrician ahead of time and see how they feel about the subject. It's always difficult to get information when you are stressed and dealing with a child that is sick. Unless you are proactive with your care provider, ninety nine point nine percent of the time you are going to receive whatever the computer spits out as the standard of care. For the last fifty years this has normally meant you were walking out of the doctor's office with a prescription for an antibiotic. Lastly, remember, anytime antibiotics are taken, be sure to follow up with an intake of acidophilus to help restore the friendly bacteria in the gut.

Points to Remember

1. Currently, there are more than eighty thousand chemicals that the FDA considers legal that we are exposed to all the time.

2. To use a Synthetic anything is an insult to the body.

3. Genetic modification is the process of forcing genes from one species into another *entirely unrelated* species.

4. Because antibiotics are so accepted, in many ways they are even more dangerous than GMOs to your health.

5. Eighty percent of your immune function originates with your intestinal flora.

10

Body and Soul Speak

As a creator, the universe is constantly reflecting back to me everything that is going on in my life. I have a hand in all of my reality and certainly this includes my health. As I have said before, there are no victims. It is an illusion. There is, however, more going on here than just the Law of Attraction at work, and this is direct communication from your Higher Self or Superconscious.

These understandings are true for all of us, parents and children alike. The Quantum children are sensitive and they are going to pick up on everything going on within the family. If there is a lot of difficulty occurring around them, especially on an emotional level, it could easily show up in a child's health.

Within this chapter, I will be touching more deeply into understandings around health and healing that conventional medicine does not address. First and foremost, we have to keep coming back to the understanding that everything is connected. Our physical body is not separate from our emotional body, mental body or any of the other subtle energy bodies that comprise the All of who we are. A problem that is created within our emotional bodies will eventually show itself somewhere within our physical body. The same thing happens with imbalances that we create within our mental body. Symptoms begin to appear and the average person might visit their doctor to get an opinion as to what is going on, and the **answer given is normally based upon a limited mechanistic concept of the human body.** The limiting model that conventional medicine has chosen only addresses the symptoms that show up in the physical body and not the true cause. *This is the equivalent of* *cutting off the top of a weed, leaving its roots alone, allowing it to grow back at a later time.*

The intriguing thing about the body is that it is always talking to us. Your body is constantly mirroring what is going on in your life. This is expected from the Law of Attraction, but there is more going on here than just the mirroring. Your higher levels of consciousness are also speaking to you through your body. The problem is that we aren't listening. You are not your body. You are a soul having a human experience using a vehicle that you know as your body. This conveyance we have chosen is amazing on so many levels, and one of the most important is that as souls we can give ourselves information through it. You are so much more than you know! I'm sure you've heard that before. Hopefully, before we are done you will begin to believe it.

The Game

In many ways, this reality we live in is like one of my fantasy computer games. When you begin the game, you enter at the lowest level and you proceed by facing challenges. In so doing you gain experience and move up to the next level. If you are with a group, each of you has your own strengths, weaknesses and abilities. Your job as the leader of the group is to maximize the strengths of your team to achieve the goals at hand. Eventually, you make your way through the game. What do you do after that but buy another game or an expanded version of the same? With each experience, your soul grows. And so it goes, game after game. You might even become so good as to be able to build your own game.

If you ever fail at a task in any of the games, it isn't the end of the world. You simply set the task aside for a while and address it at a later time when your strength is greater. As an old "gamer" you'd know how important it is to save your progress because sometimes you step into a challenge that is above your skill level, you and your team can be "wiped out." No problem, you just reset back to your last saved position and go from there. In many ways, this is a perfect analogy for reincarnation and the continuum of lifetimes that we move through.

In any game that we play, we normally start by getting to know the rules. How do I play this game? And so we spend a great deal of our childhood and adolescence trying to do just that. However, this playing field known as Earth is one of the most challenging places for us to test ourselves. Life here is like trying to slog your way through a marsh or a bog. It can be very slow going and can require a lot of effort. The veil of amnesia we move through as we incarnate is probably one of our biggest gifts and also greatest challenges that we have created for ourselves. Prior to our lifetime, we create a remarkably elaborate chart of everything that we would like to accomplish during our experience on Earth. Then we come through the veil and promptly forget every bit of it. Even though as souls we have constructed all kinds of things that we would like to accomplish in this lifetime, and have gone to great lengths to hire individuals to play different roles for us, we forget all of it as soon as we drop into the game. As a consequence, all of us in conjunction with Source, as the master creators of this game have opened up different lines of communication to help us on our adventures.

You Communicating to You

Certainly, one of the most important pieces of information you can provide for yourself is determining where you are out of balance in your life. Your physical body was set up so that it would reflect back to you everything that is going on in your life. This is a fairly passive action which is constant and ongoing. In essence, it is how the Law of Attraction is working within each of us in every moment. Our higher levels of consciousness also have the capability of being more direct with us if it wants to get our attention. Pain is, unquestionably, a wonderful attention- getter. The problem is that most of us just don't connect the dots and associate what is going on with our bodies with something greater.

145

The early messages that we receive are barely a whisper. It could be something as simple as a single cough. You and I normally would dismiss something this small, but to a Master, it could sound as loud as a blaring trumpet. The next level that we get is like a "nudge or a poke." Many of us in the intuitive field have become sensitive enough to be aware that something is afoot when this strong of a signal comes into our consciousness. Then we escalate rapidly to the "2x4 upside the head" and yes, sometimes we are so hard-headed that we need something harder like a "crowbar" instead. And finally, there is the "being run over by a truck" level of signal. Needless to say, these last two are pretty hard to ignore.

There have been quite a few excellent books on this subject. This concept is not new. Louise Hay, the founder of Hay House Publishing, wrote a small book called *Heal Your Body* all the way back in 1976 and *You can Heal Your Life* in 1984. These are still two of Hay House's bestsellers thirty plus years later. Julia Cannon, Dolores's daughter, wrote an excellent book on the subject as well. *Soul Speak: The Language of Your Body*. Dr. Michael Lincoln has an extremely comprehensive reference guide called *Messages from the Body: Their Psychological Meaning*.

For our purpose here I would like to share with you some of the understandings that Julia Cannon has given us in her book and other thoughts I have been blessed with over the years. As I mentioned earlier, I have a Master's degree that focused heavily on hypnotherapy. About a year after I completed my studies, I had the pleasure of training with Dolores and Julia Cannon in their modalities. Virtually every aspect of QHHT (Quantum Healing Hypnosis Therapy) is designed to have clients quiet their Conscious mind in order to work more directly with their higher levels of consciousness. Some people refer to this level as their "Higher Self" or "Oversoul." Dolores called it the Sub- Conscious or SC for short. It is important to note that this is not the level of the mind we refer to normally in psychology, and because I have degrees in Math and Psychology from Duke I don't like to confuse the terms, so I prefer to

146

use the term Super Conscious. There is no right or wrong way to address it. Whatever works best for you is perfect.

Big You

Most of us see ourselves as what I am going to refer to as "Little You." Separate, isolated and alone in the world.

Dolores taught QHHT around the world and many of the new practitioners had more questions about this level of consciousness they were connecting with that KNEW everything about each of us. It was during a workshop in Sydney, Australia that Julia was given a vision of it and rather emphatically told to draw it. I have to laugh at this because I have had the same thing happen to me and it can really shock or surprise you. Julia was equally surprised. Here is a simplified image of "Big You."

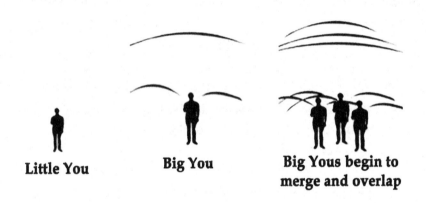

Little You   **Big You**   **Big Yous begin to merge and overlap**

Your Higher Self, Oversoul, or Super Conscious is with you all the time, and it blends with everyone else's Higher Self to form a group consciousness that knows everything about you. It is from this blending that we can say you are connected to everyone and everything on the planet.

It gets even better. "Big You" is fully blended with Source. But put yourself in Big You's shoes for a moment. How would you pass on information to you? Here you are, fully connected to Source with all the guidance you are trying to convey to yourself, but Little You passed through the veil of amnesia during the incarnation process and doesn't even remember that you exist. So how do you get Little You's attention? You could, of course, use dreams. If the vision was vivid enough it could work. You could send yourself signs that you pass every day on your way to work as a form of subliminal message. Or how about using the one thing that you are attached to every moment of every day: your body. Let's face it; it is pretty hard to ignore our bodies when things are amiss.

Direct communication is always the most preferred method when working with our SC, which is why QHHT works as well as it does. We use hypnosis to induce a level of relaxation with the intention of gently moving the conscious mind out of the way so the client can receive the guidance and healing they are looking for. Any practice that helps you quiet your mind is going to be helpful. So even if you aren't seeing the clues being provided to you, Big You has more than one way of getting its message across. And for this, the body is probably Big You's favorite backup system.

The code that is used is fairly simple once you know what to look for. So let me give you a glimpse of the manual. The simplest place to start is to think of what any particular body part does for the body. What is its function? If you have problems speaking your truth or feeling that you aren't heard, I would expect to see problems begin to manifest in the throat area. How about back trouble from carrying the weight of the world on your shoulders?

You also have to be a bit of a detective and recognize that the messages may be subtle and unique to you. We could both have a similar challenge in our lives but this does not mean our higher levels of consciousness will use the exact same message for both of us. The messages will be designed uniquely for each of us. So you have to feel for what seems right for you. It is a process I'll speak more on later in this chapter.

148

Heart and the Blood

Let's take, for example, an individual who has developed clogged arteries to his heart, creating for himself a heart attack. Conventional medicine would address the challenge from a purely physical level. They would stabilize him and then perform surgery to clean out his arteries. After this, they probably would put him on prescription medication to prevent the restrictions in his arteries from reoccurring. Quite possibly, all this is necessary at this point in the game because the individual let it get to the "run over by a truck level."

From a holistic view, blood is our life force flowing through our body. This ill individual had been squeezing it off in some area of his life and quite possibly all areas. The physical manifestation was merely the buildup of the plaque. The heart is our center of love. All our issues of self-love tend to be expressed here in some form or fashion. Even the term heart attack is a reflection of a lack of love. It is describing a situation where you are literally attacking your own heart. Doing the physical repair without the emotional repair in this instance is leaving the door open for another trip to the emergency room.

It takes time to find the root of the difficulties a person is having and the business of medicine does not want to take the time. Within the current medical model, the average doctor sees a patient for about five to six minutes at a time. If you truly want to help an individual heal on all levels, and the doctor is either unwilling or unable to fill this role, then the medical community needs to recognize this gap in their system and bring in other individuals that can. This is one of the strengths of the holistic field, and in my opinion it is vital that it be included in the conventional medical model.

Moving Forward

I had a very personal situation get my attention a few years ago. In November of 2013, as a pilot for United, I was offered an early retirement package. If I chose to accept the package, I would be walking away from a $250,000-a-year job and into an unknown career as a writer and speaker. My internal guidance was crystal clear that this was the correct path to take, and yet two weeks after I signed the papers accepting the severance package, I had a major bout of gout. Now, if you have never experienced gout, you are lucky. Imagine taking an ice pick and shoving it through your toe. A bit of a wake-up call, don't you think? This was a life-changing event I thought I had prepared for and yet here were the joints of my feet screaming at me. I knew instinctively I had lingering fears at the subconscious level that I wasn't ready for this. Our legs provide us with our support but our joints provide us with the flexibility that we need to run and move fluidly in any direction.

It took time but I addressed this both physically and emotionally. I looked at all aspects of my diet and then worked with my good friend, Dr. Debra Zepf, an integrative doctor, and her husband, Larry, to balance my energy and to reduce the inflammation. In my meditations, I was shown that the links to this ran far deeper than just an early retirement. I found unhealed issues of trust with Source and how I would be supported in this lifetime. I engaged another friend of mine, Donna Aazura, who practices a form of therapy she calls Conscious Alchemy (www.NewHumanProject.com). Her specialty is the clearing of the deep core issues that we might carry and this was exactly the assistance I needed. Most of us work on superficial issues that are on top of these core problems. But just like a house of cards, if you can clear one of the cards off the bottom, you can collapse the entire structure, clearing away all the layers above. In my situation, it took me awhile to bring everything back into balance but when I finally did, all the pain and discomfort disappeared and has not shown itself again for over two years now.

Love is the most important healing element when you are working in the emotional plane. I also had to be transparent with myself to allow these old wounds and fears to express themselves fully. Any form of suppression would only prolong the discomfort and healing. It took me about eight months to finally move into a state of gratitude and love, sufficient enough to heal my physical body. My feet still work as a barometer for me, letting me know if any of the old fears wish to show themselves again. It is possible that some residual energy might pop up from time to time. We just have to be aware and present. In doing so, we can hear and feel what our bodies are telling us.

Cancer

Cancer. Is there another single word or diagnosis that can convey so much emotion and fear? It certainly is one of our "run over by a truck" level messages. It gets people to stop and address their lives possibly for the very first time. Heart attacks used to have this kind of effect as well but since our heart surgeries and repairs have gotten better, it has allowed people to go back to their former lives. This is wonderful if the patterns that created the heart attack in the first place are healed, but frequently this is not the case.

Cancer at its core is unhealed emotional energy that has been held in the body for a long time. Left unaddressed for years, you as a soul finally move it to such a level of awareness that it can't be ignored any longer. Long-held resentments, deep hurts, hatred and anger can all at some point in time manifest into cancer. Instead of addressing the message of cancer with love, forgiveness and gratitude, we have been conditioned to go into fear and to fight against it with all our might. As I've said before, what you focus on expands.

Deep emotional wounds are never healed with a scalpel, chemotherapy or radiation. They are healed with love, forgiveness and letting go. You can do all the physical procedures you want, but if you don't address the root cause, you have merely put a Band-Aid on a foot-long gash.

151

I am only giving you a brief understanding of cancer from this perspective. Julia, in her book, devoted an entire chapter to the subject. In it, she described one of her mother's QHHT sessions with a client who had cancer. During the session, Dolores asked him if he was angry about anything. He shouted, "I hate my ex-wife. She has the children and she won't let me see them." When Dolores told him that he had to forgive her in order to let go of the anger/cancer, he replied, "I can't do that. You don't know what she's done." It certainly is pretty obvious where this is going for this gentleman.

Can you see how our victimhood mentality can hold energies such as these, locked in place? We are the creators of our reality. This man hired his wife and contracted with her to play a role in his life. We don't know everything that this man and woman were to learn from their experience together. We would have to look deeper to find that out. It could be some form of Karmic balancing from a past life or any number of other reasons. Our minds really don't need to know. When we can see it for what it is, "an opportunity to learn and grow," then we are more likely to let the emotion go and move more fully into forgiveness.

Sexuality

Many aspects of our self-image can be mirrored within our sexuality. Breast cancer, for example, can open us up to any number of issues that women face today. Self-love, lack of nurturing of self, need for perfection, over-mothering, or overprotection. Any of these might be at the root of this physical problem. What about men with impotence? Sexual pressure, guilt, and any number of other challenges could be a factor. You could even go into one's past lives and look to see if there were any vows of celibacy. Both men and women judge their bodies enormously and this is always going to filter down into our physical experience in some fashion. One of my wife's favorite sayings is, "your body is listening and it believes everything that you say about it."

152

Left and Right

Another clue that helps us get a better sense of what is coming up for us is to look at whether the problem occurs on the right side of the body or the left. This is intriguing in that it brings in three different possible meanings. Normally, we receive from our less dominant hand and give from our dominant one. Most people are right-handed, so for them issues in receiving would be reflected anywhere along the left side, and issues of giving or letting go would show up on the right. If someone is left-handed, these most likely will be flip-flopped.

Another meaning of left and right is associated with male and female. We all have both a feminine and masculine side within us. Normally, we see emotional issues within our feminine side showing up on the left and those of the masculine showing up on the right. This could also mirror a problem with a specific individual. If you had a male boss and were experiencing all kinds of frustrations working with him, I would normally expect to see some indication along your right side. Regardless of where an imbalance shows up, we constantly want to feel for what is true. Don't assume anything.

My mother was a perfect example of this male/female dynamic. Her major challenge she got to deal with during her lifetime was abandonment or lack of support from the men in her life. Mother's dad died when she was about twenty. He had remarried about two years previously and mother's experience was right out of Cinderella. It wasn't pretty. Her next male challenge occurred when my father died of lung cancer at the age of forty. I was eight years old and mother became a single mom with four kids in the early 60s. Seeing death as a form of abandonment is an interesting view, and I think you can see how we might internalize it as such. My mother remarried about six years later when I was fourteen. Tom, her second husband, had three boys. He was a nice man, a widower, but truth be told, I really feel that he was just looking for someone to help him with the boys. About a year later mother had another son, my half-brother, Chris. This brought us up to seven boys and one girl in the family. Do you think we had enough testosterone running around the house? We could practically field our own football team. Mother and Tom stayed together for about two more years before they broke up. As mother got older she had problems with her right hip, her right knee and her right ankle. Eventually, she had surgery to replace the ankle joint. It never fully healed and gave her difficulty for the rest of her life. Not a single ailment ever showed itself on her left side.

The last meaning for left and right is the most intriguing of all. The right side represents issues from this lifetime and the left our previous ones. Over her fifty year career, Dolores Cannon did thousands of sessions with clients. A session would begin with guided visualizations, followed by a past life regression and then direct work with the Super Conscious. Different levels of healing were always a priority in these sessions, and you would be surprised at the number of times that problems an individual was having were linked to a pattern they had been working on over a number of lifetimes. My daughter and I found one particular challenge she was having had connections to similar difficulties in more than ten different past lives. That hurts just to think about it.

Accidents

The last thing I would like to cover in this area is accidents, or as spirit likes to call them, "message incidents." Are you a Divine creator of your reality or not? Are you a victim of life's circumstances, or is it that you just don't know what is going on behind the scenes? Accidents are never accidents. If you aren't hearing the messages you are attempting to give yourself, accidents can be another way for you to get your attention and keep you on your chosen path.

When you receive the message fully, the healing from these "message incidents" can happen in a fraction of the "normal time," even instantaneously. I felt so strongly about this that I offered my services free of charge to the Denver Bronco's football team. What better way to prove this concept than working with young men that are constantly in a place where an injury could occur at any moment. The Broncos in 2013 had three aging veterans with a combined salary of eighteen million dollars that they had already put on injured reserve for the rest of the year with various leg and joint injuries. Do you remember what I said about the legs, especially our joints and how they can reflect our restrictions about moving forward in life? I felt that by working directly with the SC, their recovery time could be a fraction of what the doctors had predicted. The exact timing of any healing is always within the individual. For my part, I would not have touched their body in any fashion. I would be using QHHT to facilitate the work that would be done between the player and the SC. What did they have to lose, right? The Bronco's management already was conceding that these players were out for the year and the money was gone. Unfortunately, they wouldn't even agree to a meeting where I could explain more fully my proposal.

Your Car

Your car is a perfect mirroring device for your physical body. It is our most common mode of transportation. Isn't that what our body does for our soul? I had a copilot who was having challenges keeping his medical license to fly because he was having heart problems. It turns out he had just blown the motor in his truck as well.

How about getting rear ended? Could the individual getting hit in the back need a bit of a nudge to get going? Problems with a starter certainly would fall into this category as well. Perhaps if you had a weak battery it might be an indication that your energy was low as well. We are surrounded by subtle signals all the time. The question is, are we aware enough to recognize them as such? The analogies go on and on. Hopefully, the problems show themselves early and are minor because the severity of the action normally correlates with the level of the message. Along these lines, if you have to resort to a car accident to get your attention, then things have already progressed to a pretty severe level and there is something very important you need to look at.

Getting Back on Track

In her book, Julia included instances from her mother's case files where individuals had had major life-changing accidents and they wanted to know why. One individual had been an excellent athlete heading towards a possible professional career. He lost his arm while playing with rockets that were part of a science experiment. In the session, the SuperConscious revealed to him that life as a professional athlete was not his chosen path and this was his way of doing a course correction.

Another example she used was a man that had been mugged, stabbed and left to die in an alley. He managed to crawl back to the street and was taken to the hospital. In the session, the SC told him that on the spirit side, the individuals that had mugged him were his best friends and that he was deviating from his chosen path to the degree that something drastic was needed to help him. They didn't want to harm him, but they had agreed to do whatever was necessary to keep him on track.

Obviously, both of these are extreme examples of ways we can create course corrections for ourselves. Life does not move in a straight line. It is filled with twists, turns and side explorations. Virtually all of us need a course correction from time to time. Hopefully, you will be listening and yours will be of a more gentle form.

*****

Of course, not every message is tied to anger or guilt or some other strong emotion. If you are mindful of your body the subtle messages can come in when they aren't so dire. I was once playing tennis in a drill class at the local recreation center. I was just getting back after a long layoff. Towards the end of the class, I tweaked my knee a bit. As we finished, Christina, who ran the class, said that the next court over was open for a while, if we wanted to stay and continue to play a little more. This was during the winter when these indoor courts are normally booked all the time, especially Saturdays. So we took her up on her offer. I hit two more balls and felt my knee give way again. When I went within and asked what it was trying to tell me, the lyrics of an old Simon and Garfunkel song started running through my head.

> *Slow down, you move too fast*
> *You've got to make the morning last*
> *Just kicking down the cobblestones*
> *Looking for fun and feelin' groovy*

After I stopped laughing, I realized that all my body was telling me was that I had done enough for the day and it was time to stop. There was no need to overdo it.

The Process

The process of discovery is an inner one. The information is being provided to you and you are the keeper of the code. Every time you open up an inner dialogue with your higher self, you are reestablishing trust: trust of yourself and trust of your soul. The questions that you direct within and your answers are personal. There is no right or wrong way to begin. You just begin. The process is organic. It will evolve with you. There is no one way or one answer that works for everyone. Your job is to be willing to jump down that rabbit hole and see where it leads you.

As you begin the process, you must be patient as to how and when you receive your answers. You want the information to come from Big You, but under normal circumstances you are asking the questions when your conscious mind is on high alert. Dolores calls the conscious mind "Mister Stupid" for a good reason. It doesn't know anything of value. It loves to answer, but its response comes from all the surface memories and programs that exist within you. Big You, on the other hand, has access to the true wisdom that you are seeking but it won't interrupt your conscious mind. It will wait patiently for a time when your conscious mind has become quiet and then it will send the information to you. This may come while you are daydreaming or doing some mundane task. Nighttime, while you are asleep is always an excellent time to receive the information. Ask your questions right before going to sleep and just be open. Regardless of how you set yourself up to receive the information, be patient. You can't force it. Well, I guess you could try to but it won't do you any good. You will find some way to get the message across to you. Each of us has a personal journey, a personal guidance system and our own way of communicating with ourselves. Our job is to be open, aware and to listen.

The first part of the process is to receive the message. The next part is to take action. You have free will. You can listen or not. You can take action or not. But if you hear and receive the message and don't take action, it would be the same as if you didn't get the message. Trust me; you aren't the first person to be so stubborn that they didn't take any action until they took a crowbar right between their eyes. But be easy on yourself, the medical community didn't teach you this, your parents didn't, and the education system didn't. You don't know what you don't know.

Learning to Speak and to Love Your Body

Just as Big You can have an enormous effect on your physical body, the conscious you can as well. Unfortunately, in our societies today, it is far more likely that an individual is expressing judgment towards their body rather than love. Dr. Joe Dispenza has some excellent examples he constantly refers to in both his books and workshops, where individuals have reversed all kinds of major medical conditions by taking the time every day to bless their energy centers. Most of what we do is by habit and conditioning. Why not make such a beneficial practice part of your habit? Express love and gratitude to your body every chance you get and I guarantee you that it will respond in kind.

For the average person, about eighty-five percent of their daily actions are controlled by their subconscious patterns. So if you are going to consciously have an effect on your physical body, you must take action or have the thought enough times so that your subconscious beliefs and your conscious actions are on the same page. This is why it takes a while before we see changes in our body.

Have you ever thought of what would occur if you spoke to your body from the perspective of Source? Most of us have been conditioned so much that we can't even conceive of it. And yet as I've said before "you are Divine." You are this amazing creator being who is having a human experience. One of the QHHT practitioners did just that and she posted her story on our forum:

"Every winter I seem to come down with a bad flu or cold. My symptoms are chills, cold feet, a mild fever, and congestion with lots of drippy mucous that lasts for a minimum of three weeks. This weekend we returned from Oregon and I felt the symptoms coming on strong, so the next day I decided to see if I could prevent the flu from overtaking my body. I said, 'Attention bacteria and viruses in my body, this is God speaking to you, and I want to let you know how much you are loved and how grateful I am for your presence to teach me how to heal myself. You have done your job, and I am now going to release you with much love and thanks and gratitude. You may now travel to the light to continue your journey with much love and much thanks.' I then imagined them as tiny specks of color traveling out of my body through a golden/white light doorway. I repeated this twice and then several times throughout the day and for the next couple of days. **It truly worked**, and other than cold feet, I feel wonderful and did not develop any other symptoms!"

From a quantum perspective, our physical bodies are pure energy. In essence, they are information that has been expressed into a physical form. What better type of information can we add to the field that is creating this body than love and gratitude?

Points to Remember

1. When you address a problem from only the physical side of things, it is the equivalent of *cutting off the top of a weed, leaving its roots alone, allowing it to grow back at a later time.*

2. Your higher levels of consciousness are speaking to you through your body.

3. Certainly one of the most important pieces of information you can provide for yourself is where you are out of balance in your life.

4. Your physical body was set up so that it would reflect back to you everything that is going on in your life.

5. The code that is used is fairly simple once you know what to look for. The simplest place to start is to think of what any particular body part does for the body.

11

Information Fields of the Body

The informational fields of the body are yet another area of study that pharmaceutical-based medicine completely ignores. Changes in these fields take place outside of space and time. Healing can be instantaneous. There are no side effects and the therapies associated with informational medicine can work just as effectively for a one-pound baby as they would for a two hundred fifty-pound man.

We are vibrational beings living in a vibrational universe, yet none of this understanding has filtered itself into conventional medicine. Why? One could look at the business side of medicine, which has done everything in its power to block any modality or form of treatment that does not come from the pharmaceutical or surgical model. Furthermore, it has done it so well that the business of medicine is now the number one industry in terms of profit in our country. One would think that it would be oil and gas, but actually it is the medical industry. I've often wondered what medicine would look like today if Big Money had not taken control of it. What if the only thing that mattered was the healing? And yet, even putting the cost differential aside (allopathic medicine is considered to be twenty times more expensive than its alternative counterparts), I don't think you or I would mind if the current model truly was one of Wellness; unfortunately, it is one that simply manages illness.

Those who control the business side of this industry have been hugely effective at blocking anything they see as competition, but there is more to it than just that. Group consciousness has a great deal to do with it as well. You are conditioned to believe that the man in the white coat has all the answers; consequently, you don't look elsewhere. You vote with your dollar and the choices you make. Energy and informational medicine are the future of medicine, and allopathic medicine is more than one hundred years behind where it should be in this area. From a group consciousness point of view, we are just as responsible for this as they are because we allowed it to occur.

There are ten major dogmas that the scientific community holds dear. They hold these interesting points of view not just as a theory but as a Truth. And as I mentioned earlier, just because something is held as a belief does not make it true. The scientific method has always been about exploration and openness to all thought. Nevertheless, somewhere along the way many of the early thoughts that formed the basis of what is known as "scientific materialism" moved from being a point of view to belief and then to dogma. Rupert Sheldrake, a Biology professor at Cambridge University in England, is the author of thirteen different books. His last two, "*The Science Delusion*" and "*Science set Free*" both do a wonderful job discussing these dogmas in depth.

Throughout the Middle Ages, there was a lot of conflict between the Church and the budding fields of science. A mutually beneficial truce was formed between the two, based on the theories advanced by Rene Descartes. Descartes was a French philosopher, mathematician, and scientist who was born in 1596 and died in 1650 at the age of fifty four. His view was that **ONLY** the human mind, God and the angels have consciousness. Everything else he considered as just **MATTER**. This theory also included the belief that all matter was therefore devoid of consciousness or purpose. Science was given as its domain the study of matter and its laws; included within this was our physical body. The Church would be in charge of consciousness, the soul and God.

Descartes's point of view was that all the matter in the universe was just stuff. Animals were just machines. Plants were just machines and the human body was just a machine. Descartes's view stressed that only humans have consciousness; therefore, we could do

162

whatever we wanted with everything else. Certainly all the abuses that humanity has heaped on the Earth, plants and animal kingdoms over the last four hundred years are reflective of this.

It goes further than this, however. Consciousness could only be housed within your mind. Therefore, all forms of memory or other forms of thought had to reside strictly within the brain. No form of group consciousness existed. All awareness became separate, and any form of intuitive connection that a person might have with another was seen as just an illusion. From this point of view, even a mother's intuitive connection with her child was not a real connection. It had to be explained away as something that really wasn't valid.

So, even though most aspects of his theories on consciousness and matter have been disproved over the last one hundred years, they still form the basis of scientific and medical thought today. To the medical community, your consciousness has no effect on what is going on in your body. It is strictly a physical cause and effect, and your body is treated as if it were a machine. If a part fails or is broken, an individual could simply change it medically. Every part is isolated until we get down to a single cell, and then we go to the elements within a cell and finally we get to the genes and the DNA. Scientists believed at the time that everything was determined by our genes and our DNA and that they were fixed. Hence, the concept became known as Genetic Determinism.

The Human Genome Project (1990-2003) was a child born from this theory. The business of medicine hoped to map and isolate what they thought at the time would be hundreds of thousands of genes that make up our body, thinking a single gene might be associated with a solitary function. The thought was that if you had a problem in your body there would be a single gene associated with it. In so doing they would be able to control or patent the gene that would fix the problem, and then, of course, charge you for it. The problem was their assumption was completely wrong. Approximately twenty-five thousand genes were mapped during the project—far fewer than the amount that was expected to express the vastness of the human experience. In the chimpanzee genome project, it was found their genes were virtually identical to ours. They have the same kinds of proteins and genes that we do. You could hardly tell the difference. What we have found since then, through the study of epigenetics, is that genes combine in an almost infinite number of ways to create the astonishing variety of life that exists.

It might be natural for you to assume that the chimpanzee's genome would be similar to ours, but would you also believe the fruit fly also has many of the same genes? Our DNA is more complex, but many of the core structures were the same.

So if you can't explain the differences by genes, what then? The answer to this question is what biologists call morphogenetic fields. These are fields of information which regulate and determine how different genes will be combined, as well as which genes will be switched on or off. Our genes are like the building blocks of our structure. They are the bricks and the cement. The morphogenetic fields are holographic fields that hold the information which tells your body how to use those genes. We use the same building materials all the time to construct all kinds of different buildings. The only thing different is the blueprint.

Morphogenetic fields (The Living Matrix, 2009)

There is a hierarchy of fields organizing our bodies. There is a field for the body, one for the organs, one for the tissues and one for the cells. Fields, in general, are intrinsically holistic. By this, I mean they can't be cut or divided without re-forming as whole fields. Have you ever tried to cut a slice out of the gravitational field? You can't. If you cut a single magnet into a hundred different pieces, each will have a fully formed and complete field. If it were a machine, this wouldn't happen. You would only get a broken machine.

Biologists have been studying morphogenetic fields since the 1920s. The concept is not new. Because these fields are non-physical and vary in size, one person's field can interact with another's. Add to this the concept that our consciousness can move outside of space and time and it is not much of a stretch to imagine the same for these fields as well. This opens up whole new ways for us to look at how we interact with the universe.

The HeartMath Institute in California has done some fascinating research over the last several decades. They did an experiment where a subject was shown at random, different pictures on a computer monitor. Each picture was chosen by a random number algorithm so that even the computer didn't know what picture would be displayed next. Each subject was wired up to measure everything going on in their body. The pictures used in the study were deliberately chosen to evoke an emotional response: pictures of a poisonous snake in mid-strike; a horrific car crash; puppies playing; a toddler smiling, and so forth. I was brought up to believe everything simply moves from our senses to the brain and one could expect to see the earliest responses in the brain, but that wasn't the case. **The images were registered in the heart,** and more intriguing than this, they were registered **before** they were shown on the computer. A part of each subject's consciousness was working outside of space and time, with the information flowing from the heart to the brain and then to the body.

Some of our most intriguing work occurs when we can affect directly these different fields of information. I believe that many of the instantaneous healings we have had over the millenniums are a result of radical and sudden changes in an individual's information field. Along these lines, one of the ways of looking at disease is as scrambled or disrupted information being provided to the body. Another term for this is "incoherent information." Fix the incoherence and the body will respond accordingly. Needless to say, this is radically different from the way conventional medicine addresses the body. Even though the new science of epigenetics has proven otherwise, many doctors and scientists still hold onto the old belief that our DNA and genes control everything. This is another belief through which we could express our victimhood mentality, seeing ourselves as slaves or victims to the body that our parents gave us if nothing was changeable.

One of the best examples of spontaneous healing that you can actually see comes from Gregg Braden. Gregg is a New York Times best-selling author of numerous books. He is internationally known as a pioneer in bridging science, spirituality and the real world. The YouTube link below demonstrates quantum healing by thought alone, accomplished at a drug-free hospital in Beijing, China. The woman involved had a three inch inoperable tumor from bladder cancer and we can see it dissolve in real-time on an ultrasound screen. This particular video was part of a talk that Gregg delivered in Italy in 2007.

Gregg Braden, Bladder Cancer dissolves in less
than three minutes using The Language of Emotion
https://youtu.be/GUbEgg6GklU

The power of thought and focused feelings cannot be overstated. The practitioners, as well as the woman, were all focused on feelings of being in a healthy body in the present moment; consequently, a shift happened within the quantum field.

Highly evolved Yogis and Tibetan Monks have demonstrated for thousands of years these types of healing. Jesus, in his time,

166

performed numerous healings in much the same manner. Masters such as these would hold within their consciousness an image of wholeness and health that replaced the incoherent information that was causing the disease or other imbalances in the body. The physical universe would then change to mirror the new blueprint. At a deeper level of understanding is the fact that a master such as Jesus did not heal anyone. Jesus opened up the space for the healing but the individual had to step into that space in order to complete the healing. If an individual had a karmic attachment to an illness or some other form of soul-level contract, the affliction could not be healed. It would violate the soul's choice.

I talked about Dr. Joe Dispenza back in Chapter 4. He healed his broken back by drawing in his mind over and over every vertebra in his body in perfect alignment and health. It took him months to accomplish it but eventually he was able to move into a state of consciousness where the only thing that existed for him was a healthy spine. In essence, what had occurred was that he had been able to create a whole new set of information within his field. Needless to say, you can't go through an experience like that and not be changed. Understanding how healing like that takes place became his life's work. His books, *You are the Placebo, Evolve Your Mind,* and *Breaking the Habit of Being Yourself* are all wonderful places to begin delving into this subject more deeply if you choose.

If you get a chance, please attend one of his workshops. Dr. Joe begins every workshop with a guided meditation where you bless each of your energy centers. The power of this practice is undeniable. He can cite case after case of individuals that have changed their lives by doing this simple practice on a daily basis. Individual meditation is always wonderful but doing a group meditation where, say, three hundred individuals are all blessing their bodies is truly a remarkable experience.

In her forty plus years of practicing QHHT, Dolores Cannon described various healings that occurred during her sessions. She once had a woman with a curvature of the spine walk out of the session four inches taller, her spine completely straightened. Most of the healing in these sessions occurs over time because in many instances we still have some work to do, but this doesn't mean it can't be instantaneous. In QHHT we work directly with SuperConscious and as I said before, this level of consciousness is fully connected to the Divine. When changes occur for the client, they happen in the quantum field and are then translated into the body and we get to see and feel the results.

During my flying career, I logged more than twenty three thousand hours of flight time, more than half of those flights being long international routes with enormous shifts in circadian rhythms. Dealing with jet lag and the length of time it would take each of us to recover has always been an important aspect of each crew member's quality of life. One way of looking at this is that the information running these rhythms gets disrupted. For my Master's thesis, I conducted a study with flight attendants and pilots using a form of light and sound technology that created deep states of relaxation in the body regardless of the time of day. This technology had been proven to create amazing states of homeostasis. In essence, it was sending coherent information to their fields. I tracked each pilot's and flight attendant's sleep cycles for three months. On average they recovered thirty to forty percent faster from their trips by simply placing coherent information in their fields once or twice a day.

Even though we have been studying these fields for almost one hundred years, in many ways I feel like we are in kindergarten in regard to our level of true understandings in this area. This section was meant to introduce this subject to you. If you would like to explore it further, some of the best sources I can offer you on this subject are the 2009 film documentary, *The Living Matrix*. It is about the new science of healing. Lynne McTaggert's book, *The Field* and Dr. Rupert Sheldrake's books and YouTube videos are also excellent. Dr. Sheldrake is truly one of the world's leading authorities on this subject.

Points to Remember

1. The current medical model is not one of Wellness; unfortunately it is one that simply manages illness.

2. To the medical community, your consciousness has no effect on what is going on in the body. Physical cause and effect is its primary focus.

3. Morphogenetic fields are fields of information that regulate and determine how different genes will be combined, as well as which genes will be switched on or off in our bodies.

4. Many of the instantaneous healings we have had over the millenniums are a result of radical and sudden changes in an individual's information field.

5. One of the ways of looking at disease is as scrambled or disrupted information that is being provided to the body. Another term for this is "incoherent information." Fix the incoherence and the body will respond accordingly.

12

Imprints and Homeopathy

Homeopathy represents an excellent modality that every parent should be aware of and utilize in the care of their families. The concept that an energetic imprint can have the same effect on the body or even a better one than a physical substance has actually been around for over two hundred years.

The new children are bringing in unusual sensitivity as part of the new levels of consciousness. For decades, we all have been exposed to synthetic products which have a hugely detrimental effect on our health. The sensitivities of the new children magnify exponentially the negative effects of these products. In this section, I want to give you a deeper understanding of homeopathy and how the body works with informational styles of medicine.

Think of water and all of its magical properties. As I mentioned earlier, my wife has a PhD in Natural Medicine and for her dissertation, she studied water. More specifically, she studied the vitalization of water. We traveled around the globe and had a chance to meet and work with some of the world's authorities on water, such as Dr. Gerald Pollack, Dr. Mae-Wan Ho in England and Masaru Emoto from Japan. Anybody that has ever had their spouse do a PhD knows what I'm talking about when I say that I might as well have been getting the Ph. myself.

To say water is mysterious is an understatement. It is life held in this remarkable liquid crystalline matrix. It is essential for all life and we use it in many different ways and yet we barely understand it. One of its properties that have been studied extensively is the fact that **water has memory**. It has been proven water receives and makes an imprint of any substance it comes in contact with. It has also shown that it can **store, record and transfer** this information! Russian and European scientists have been working in this area for more than 60 years. Another finding is the structure of water seems to be more important than the chemical composition. Water clusters work as "memory chips" like a computer. Tests have shown that it is capable of recording up to four hundred forty thousand bits of information (Popova, 2008).

Masaru Emoto, a Japanese scientist, discovered that water, as a consciousness, responds to many external influences such as different types of music, the words we utter, and even the thoughts we think. In his book, *Messages from Water*, he displays hundreds of images of frozen water crystals. Some of the images show how the water reacted when exposed to either a positive or negative energy. Some pictures displayed some very interesting before and after effects where you can see the power of prayer. We are creatures who are made up mostly of water, and Dr. Emoto's work describes beautifully the effects many of our thoughts and feelings create within our bodies.

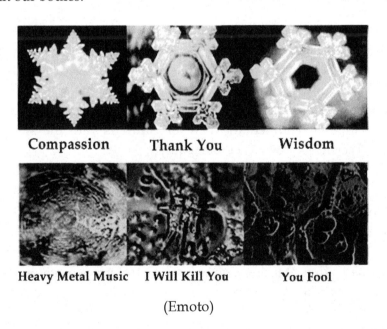

Compassion   Thank You   Wisdom

Heavy Metal Music   I Will Kill You   You Fool

(Emoto)

Emoto found that pure water forms beautiful hexagonal structures. Polluted water structures tend to be incomplete or form irregular dark shapes. Tap water in cities subjected to chlorine treatment or are heavily polluted failed to form crystals and had no signs of the characteristic hexagonal (six fold) symmetry of snowflakes.

The retentive capacity of water has been a controversial subject for many years. Mainstream science still holds tight the perspective that chemical compounds must be present to influence biological functions. And yet Dr. Bruce Lipton, a former Cellular Biology professor at Stanford University and the University of Wisconsin, found in his research that our *cells are one hundred times more receptive to energy and information than they are to chemicals* (Lipton, 2008).

Homeopathy has used and worked with the concept that water has memory since its origin in the 1800s. For those not familiar with Homeopathy, it is a quantum medical system based on the concept that **like cures like**.

Like cures like has its origins dating over two thousand years ago all the way back to Hippocrates and Paracelsus. Many cultures, including the Mayans, Chinese, Greeks, Native American Indians, and Asian Indians (Frazer, 1922) have used this model in their healing over the millenniums. It was Samuel Hahnemann though, n the 1800s, that codified the **Law of Similars** into the systematic medical science known as Homeopathy.

Homeopathy

Homeopathy became spectacularly popular in the United States and Europe in the 1800s and its strongest advocates included European royalty, American entrepreneurs, literary giants and religious leaders. Mother Teresa was a strong advocate and had a free homeopathic dispensary as one of her facilities in Calcutta. Even John D. Rockefeller, whose money and influence created the drug-centered version of medicine that we have today, had as his physician a homeopath and lived to an age of ninety nine. Currently, more than thirty million people in Europe have used or are using homeopathic products (Ullman, n.d.)

The history of homeopathy begins with the discoveries of its founder, Samuel Hahnemann (1755-1843), a German physician. Hahnemann first coined the word "homeopathy" ("homoios" in Greek means *similar*, "pathos" means *suffering*) to refer to the pharmacological principle, the Law of Similars that is its basis.

Classical homeopathic remedies are made by taking a small dose of a substance and diluting it over and over until all you have left is the essence of the substance. Chamomilia homeopathic, as an example, is created by taking chamomile flowers and mixing them in a solution to create an initial tincture. Sometimes, the initial substance may need to be ground to make the solution, sometimes not. It depends on the product that the homeopathic is being made from. Once a host tincture is formed, the product is diluted over and over again until you have only the essence or energy of the original substance remaining (Hoffman, 2009).

Let's say that a child had roundworms. The homeopathic would be made from ground roundworms mixed into a solution that at the end would carry no physical molecules of the original physical worms. This homeopathic would then stimulate the body to react and fight the roundworms inside the child. This is why we say that like cures like.

Belladonna is a classic homeopathic designed to help an individual who is suffering from poison-like symptoms. Belladonna is a very poisonous plant and if consumed would make your body tense, and give you a stomach ache as well as a fever. The homeopathic version, however, has only the energy or essence of the Belladonna and is designed to help someone recover from the exact same effects that consuming the original plant might cause.

One of the most fascinating examples of what happens in the body with a homeopathic is a story about a postman that I received from Gisela Hoffman. I had a chance to interview Gisela about homeopathy and natural healing and I will be sharing some of her thoughts with you in this section as well as in the appendix.

> **Gisela Hoffman,** daughter of **Hanna Kroeger,** who was cited as "*one of the six top holistic healers of the twentieth century*," observed her mother as she created a health food store in the 1950s, a healing retreat, an herbal company, a church, and a healing ministry. Gisela had a number of careers before she finally took over her mother's work when she passed away in 1998. She still runs Hanna's Herb Shop and The Peaceful Meadow Retreat in Boulder, Colorado.

The postman

A postman in England was delivering his mail one day when a swarm of bees attacked him. He had hundreds of bee stings on his body. Fortunately, a doctor heard his screams and came to his aid. The doctor administered a shot to prevent anaphylactic shock. I would assume that it was epinephrine but I don't know for sure.

Now this represents both the good aspects of allopathic medicine and the bad. On the good side, the doctor stabilized the postman, which was necessary at the time. However, the postman still had the toxin from the bee stings in his body. His body had to find ways to rid itself of the poison or it would have to cope by storing the toxins somewhere else. If not removed, other problems would occur and that is exactly what happened.

The bee stings healed and he was fine until a few months later when he developed a severe case of rheumatoid arthritis. So he went to his physician who gave him steroids for the arthritis. It took about a year, but eventually the symptoms of arthritis were suppressed.

Once again he was fine for another few months and then developed severe depression where no drugs helped. Prozac,

Valium, whatever. As a consequence, he had to eventually quit his job.

By now it was approximately five or six years since he had gotten stung and he decided to go and see a homeopath. She got his history and found out what was going on. She recommended a homeopathic for bee stings called Apis Mound. Nothing was given to him for the arthritis or depression. He was given a dose of the homeopathic in the office as well as a supply that he took home. Within two days his depression had lifted, completely gone. He very happily checked in with the homeopath. She was pleased and told him to keep doing what he was doing. Two weeks later the arthritis came back in full force and once again the homeopath said not to change a thing. Don't suppress it. Sure enough, after a month, the rheumatoid arthritis went away. Soon after, he woke up one morning with about two hundred bee stings all over his body. All of the previous stings magically reappeared and they were itching horribly. Once again the homeopath said to do nothing. Six hours later everything was clear and the problems never reoccurred.

All along, the postman's immune system was trying to get rid of the toxin. It was trying to do whatever it could to push it out of the body. This is true for any toxin in our bodies. When we suppress symptoms, as is the case with many practices of allopathic medicine, the immune response is blocked and stuck. A homeopathic remedy such as the one used in this instance unsticks the immune system and gets it going again.

*****

Homeopathy, more than any other modality, has been fought by the allopathic community, not because it's a poor treatment, but rather, a very beneficial one and therefore seen as its greatest competitor.

Homeopathy posed a serious threat to entrenched medicine. Orthodox physicians criticized herbalists, midwives, and other "non-regular" practitioners because they were not medically trained.

Homeopaths, however, could not be discredited as being unlearned, since they were graduates of the same medical schools as "regular" physicians. They were the integrative physicians of their time.

Although homeopathy was particularly popular among the educated and upper classes, it also had an even better reputation among the poor. Probably, the most important reason for this was its success in treating the various infectious epidemic diseases that raged throughout America and Europe during the 1800s. Statistics indicate that the death rates in homeopathic hospitals from these epidemics were a fraction of those in orthodox medical hospitals. Cincinnati homeopaths were so successful in treating people during the 1849 cholera epidemic that homeopaths published a daily list of their patients in the newspaper, giving names and addresses of those who were cured and those who died. Only three percent of the 1,116 homeopathic patients died, while between forty eight and sixty percent of those under orthodox medical treatment died. In 1878 a yellow fever epidemic raged through the Southern United States. Once again, those under homeopathic care suffered only a fraction of the deaths of those under orthodox medical care. (Ullman D. , 1987)

Besides offering effective treatment for infectious diseases, homeopaths provided care for a wide range of acute and chronic diseases. The observation that patients under homeopathic care lived longer even led some life insurance companies to offer a ten percent discount to homeopathic patients.

The training of 19th-century homeopaths compared favorably to that of their orthodox physician colleagues. Most homeopaths attended orthodox medical schools. Eventually, they developed their own medical schools or maintained departments of homeopathy within other medical schools. Boston University, University of Michigan, University of Minnesota, Hahnemann Medical College, and the University of Iowa were some of the schools teaching homeopathy. Historians today consider the education offered at the homeopathic medical colleges on a par with the orthodox medical schools of the day.

Homeopathy's popularity in the United States was obvious and yet, when reading most books on the history of American medicine, we find little or no mention of it. When there *is* a reference, it is generally derogatory, delegating homeopathy to an anomaly in medicine, a cult that ultimately disappeared, a science of placeboes rather than "real drugs," or a medical heresy. It has been said that history is written by the victors, not the defeated.

Energetic Signatures

The arguments put forth by most skeptics and nay-sayers are normally based on the belief that it requires something physical to create a healing response in the body. But it has been proven over and over again scientifically that an energetic signature of a substance can have the same result as the physical agent in the body without any of the toxic side effects. The only problem is this concept has enormous ramifications for the drug industry. You see, a homeopathic remedy costs fractions in comparison to a pharmaceutical drug and can't be patented. Needless to say, neither of these makes the drug companies happy. As you can imagine, any breakthroughs in scientific understanding in this area have normally been attacked instead of being heralded, as Jacques Benveniste discovered thirty five years ago.

Dr. Benveniste was a classically trained immunologist in France. He was studying antihistamines at the time. Our blood has small granule-shaped particles known as histamines associated with the white blood cells. These histamines are a natural part of our immune response. When we trigger our allergic reactions it is these little guys who go to work and go after the dust, pollen, or whatever we might be sensitive to. We then get those symptoms of dry itchy eyes, runny nose, etc. It is an antihistamine that blocks the histamine response. In Dr. Benveniste's research, he would color the histamines in a patient's blood and observe their reaction to the antihistamine agent that he was studying. If the agent worked, the colored histamine granules would not show up in the blood.

A colleague of his was a trained homeopath and suggested he try his experiment with a diluted sample of his agent. Initially, Dr. Benveniste was very resistant to the idea but finally conceded. They began working with the agent and finally got the solution to a point where scientifically there were no molecules of the original agent in the solution. Dr. Benveniste was stunned and astounded the solution that only housed the energetic signature of the agent had the exact same effect as his original experiments. He had his work replicated by three independent research teams, peer reviewed and published.

Even though his intention was not to validate homeopathy, in many ways that was exactly what his research had done. To say that the backlash was enormous is an understatement. He was attacked in every form possible in order to discredit him. Even though in 2000, four different independent research teams in France, Belgium, Italy and Holland under Professor Roberfroid at Belgium's Catholic University in Louvain, Brussels, once again replicated his work, the medical community still denies its validity. We have been conditioned to believe that science would always embrace new understandings and the furthering of our knowledge, but the reality is that where egos, reputations and money are involved, the status quo will fight tooth and nail to maintain its power.

More recently, Nobel Prize winner, Dr. Luc Montagnier presented some of his work at the United Nations. Dr. Montagnier is known for the level of precision and rigor that he employs in his work. What he did was to create, or more accurately, teleport DNA from one sample of solution into a completely hermetically sealed sample of **pure water**. This water had absolutely no DNA in it, and yet after his process, the water that was completely isolated had the exact same DNA that his original sample had. Whereas Dr. Benveniste had worked at the biological level, Dr. Montagnier's findings are taking us all the way to the molecular level. This fact has huge ramifications for those who believe there has to be some form of physical contact in order for something like this to occur.

Dr. Montagnier's research is cutting-edge and yet it turns out that the Russians had been working in this area since the 1950s. They called these fields of energy "torsion fields," and just like Dr. Montagnier's research, the Russians found that these fields had the ability to transport waves of information through space and time. Because it was classified information, we never heard anything about it. They were able to turn diseased tissue into healthy tissue and healthy tissue into diseased. If you would like to look at this science more closely, David Wilcock features some of this material in his New York Times bestseller, *The Source Field Investigations*.

Money and Power

Had men, money and power not fought to block homeopathic medicine at the turn of the century, our medical landscape would be vastly different today. I believe that energy and vibrational medicine would have replaced the drugs and chemistry-based products at the heart of allopathic medicine. Individuals such as Royal Rife would have been revered instead of attacked mercilessly by the American Medical Association (AMA). In case you aren't familiar with Dr. Rife, he was a genius who developed a microscope in the 1920s, decades ahead of its time. Also, he discovered that everything had a vibration and frequency and if you could balance that frequency with another one, imbalances and diseases in the body could be cured. The concept became known as the Rife frequencies. Instead of embracing his breakthroughs, the AMA did everything in its power to destroy and discredit him. Follow the money.

Everything is energy. Everything has a vibration and a frequency and as our vibration gets higher, as is the case for the Quantum children, it is much easier for us to help them using vibrational and informational medicine versus the synthetics of the drug industry.

Vibrations and the Science of Energy Medicine

Vibrational medicine or energy medicine is based on the scientific principle that all matter vibrates at a precise frequency. By using

179

resonant vibration, water can be balanced and restored. Resonance also works on the principle that like attracts like. When the C string of a harp or piano is struck, all the other octave strings of C begin to vibrate. They resonate with one another. The different parts of our physical, emotional, mental and spiritual being resonate at various frequencies of vibration. Each part of our body resonates at a specific frequency. One may think chaos would ensue but nature in her infinite wisdom has built in cycles. Each cycle has the ability to add and complement an existing frequency.

Vibrational/Energy Therapy gently invites stuck energy to move or vibrate again. When we are over-stimulated, it invites stillness. Over time, it is possible to find a balance between the two by being able to move through the entire range of possibilities fluidly. The language of vibration and resonance is expressed through the five senses. It includes color, light, crystals and gems, sound, aroma, sacred geometry and touch. Like an orchestra, your system may be deficient in a single note and consequently be thrown out of balance.

Vibrations are present in every aspect of nature. Light and sound waves are the most familiar most people think about when they use the term "vibrational." Many other forms of vibrating energy make up the electromagnetic spectrum: radio waves, television broadcasts, X-rays, cosmic rays, ultrasonic rays, infrared, cell phone transmissions, photons and microwaves. Modern physics tells us that each of these forms vibrates or oscillates at a different frequency. Hence, vibrational medicine refers to an evolving viewpoint that takes into account all forms and frequencies of the vibrating energy that contribute to the "multidimensional" human energy system. (Gerber, 2000).

The liquid crystalline structure of the human body and all biological life was designed to absorb and respond to vibratory energy. This is possible because life is predominantly water. It is the ideal carrier. When water is structured, it delivers this information easily. When water carries a broad spectrum of natural frequencies it is able to maintain coherence. Its message is strong and able to resist negative influences. Just as electrical wiring carries the electrons that produce light, water carries signals within the human body as though there were water wires connecting every molecule to other molecules (MJ Pangman, 2011).

So What Does all of this Mean to you as a Parent?

Yes, we live in a toxic environment, but it doesn't mean we stop living. You are going to do the best you can in any moment and make changes whenever possible. The most important thing you need to do in regard to your health and that of your child's is to **OWN IT**. You need to take your power back and recognize that you are the creator of your reality and certainly your health is part of it.

I've talked about how thoughts create reality and how blessing and loving your body is one of the best practices you could possibly do. I've talked about how your body is constantly a messenger for *Big You*, and how it is constantly mirroring what is going on in your life. If a problem occurs on a level other than a physical one, the cure must come from that level as well.

We are vibrational beings living in a vibrational universe, and as a consequence, the informational fields of our body are important in every aspect of our health. You might be familiar with the phrase "garbage in, garbage out." Keeping the information in these fields coherent is one of the easiest ways to maintain your natural wellness and yet it is completely ignored by conventional medicine. To allopathic medicine, preventive medicine means "early testing." This doesn't prevent anything. It merely gets you into their prescription model sooner. As I mentioned previously, Bruce Lipton, PhD, MD found that the cells of the body are more than one hundred times more receptive to energy and information than chemicals and other synthetic products.

I don't want you to disregard allopathic medicine. On the contrary, there will be times when it will be absolutely necessary. What I do believe is we all need to be more discerning and educated about our options. Medical professionals are individuals that I hire.

181

They work for me, not the other way around. If they don't listen to me and my wishes, I fire them. In general, I want to know my options based on the modalities that each professional might be familiar with.

It is still up to you to feel what is right for you and your family. Be aware of how much you are being conditioned. Instead of consulting a purely allopathic doctor, you might consider talking to an integrative one. If you don't have one available, talk to your regular doctor and perhaps a homeopath, acupuncturist or chiropractor. They could possibly help direct you to other options that might be beneficial for you to consider. There are many options available to you but don't expect the business of medicine to recommend them. As long as that side of the industry sees the alternatives as competitors and not cooperative complements, it is going to be up to you to be more proactive.

*****

It was my intention to include an in-depth piece on vaccines within this book but I feel that at this time there is still too much fear and conditioning around the subject for my message to be heard. However, I will offer a few understandings that will be beneficial to you.

First of all, you are never a victim. Exposure to an infectious disease is never a guarantee that you will become sick, just as a vaccine can never guarantee immunity. Immunity has always been a false claim made by the pharmaceutical companies. I certainly do not know if any particular product will be beneficial to you but *Big You* knows. Learn how to work with *Big You* and tap into your own answers.

There are many ways to boost a child's immune system residing within the homeopathic area that don't involve the use of toxic chemicals. Become informed; you empower yourself when you do.

*****

Government of Switzerland Deems
Homeopathy as "Legitimate Medicine"

On Tuesday, March 29, 2016 the interior ministry of the Swiss government announced its intention to elevate five complementary therapies, including homeopathy to the same level as conventional medicine. Homeopathy, holistic medicine, herbal medicine, acupuncture and traditional Chinese medicine will acquire the same status as conventional medicine by May 2017. As such they will all be covered under the insurance programs of Switzerland.

Points to Remember

1. For decades we all have been exposed to synthetic products that have a huge detrimenta effect on our health. The sensitivities of the new children magnify exponentially the negative effects of these products.

2. **Cells are one hundred times more receptive to energy and information than they are to chemicals**

3. Homeopathy is a quantum medical system based on the concept that **like cures like**.

4. Homeopathy, more than any other modality, has been fought by the allopathic community, not because it's a poor treatment, but rather, a very beneficial one and therefore seen as its greatest competitor.

5. Everything is energy. Everything has a vibration and a frequency, and as our vibration gets higher, as is the case for the Quantum children, it is much easier for us to help them using vibrational and informational medicine versus the synthetics of the drug industry.

6. The most important thing you need to do in regard to your health and that of your child's is to ___OWN IT___.

Section 4
Parenting

13

Father Knows Best

Children will always need our nurturing and support, but they are not blank slates coming into a physical lifetime. The Quantum children are highly advanced souls that are here to help all of humanity move into a new reality. As parents, we are operating in an unknown territory. We need to move into a new level of flexibility with all of our parenting. So consider this: Are you willing to throw everything you know about parenting out the window and take a different trajectory just because the moment calls for it?

I was born in September of 1954 and one month after my birthday, the TV show *Father Knows Best,* starring Robert Young and Jane Wyatt, started its ten year run. This show portrayed a Norman Rockwell ideal of what the family should look like. Then, we later had **programs** like *Leave it to Beaver* and *Walt Disney's Wonderful World of Color,* followed up by the myriad of sitcoms through the 60s, 70s and 80s that each displayed family life in their own unique way. Needless to say, things have changed since then, but you would be surprised as to how many of these images still reside within societies' unconscious. The reason I highlighted the word *program* is because that is what a TV show does within your subconscious. It conditions us. This is true for any image that we see over and over again.

Of course, some of these were beneficial and some were not. I'm sure that if you went through all the advertisements over the years you would find a predominance of products that today we consider unhealthy. My generation grew up with cigarette ads being shown all day long on virtually every show. Many of them featured a medical doctor telling how he preferred his brand over another. It took decades to get these cigarette ads to be stopped. The practice of subconscious manipulation still continues today.

Oftentimes, thoughts, concepts and beliefs in one period are beneficial to the individuals of that era but at a later time become negative. This is because of the structures in society and the consciousness of the world at the time. Some of the concepts and beliefs of the past are still beneficial today, but others, as with all structures, are in need of changing and to be let go of. Back then, there was a middle class and eighty percent to ninety percent of the mothers could afford to stay at home and take care of the family. In 2014, of the thirty four million American families with children, sixty percent had both parents working to make ends meet. Notwithstanding the economics of today, in many ways, we still parent the way we were parented and this means it is done with some form of structure.

In the past, parenting was a blend of nurturing and managing. It was assumed that the children really didn't know what was best for them and consequently had to be guided and managed in order to succeed. If a child had an interest outside of society's norms, it was almost always discouraged by the parents. At best it might have been tolerated as a hobby but never as a career. If the child persisted, then a parent not understanding the child's fascination might turn to a more passive-aggressive style and demand to know when he or she was going to stop wasting their time.

In many ways, our children are considered a reflection of us. If a mother's children succeeded, she felt good about herself. Each generation over the years has had its unique concept of what that might look like. For my generation, mothers loved the thought that their son might be a doctor, a lawyer or some other professional. Having your children healthy and happy was an afterthought. If their sons succeeded in their careers, then they would be happy. If their daughter married well and had a family, then they would be happy. The concept that each individual as a soul might actually have coded within them what they wished to experience in a lifetime never ever entered the picture. "Father knows best" was the theme of the day, and children were managed and guided into specific areas regardless of whether they truly had an interest.

Children will always need our nurturing and support. This is always going to be important, but the managing aspect of parenting needs to be diminished greatly. Our job as parents is to support the highest potential of our children and **allow them their path**. Each of us has gifts that we are bringing into a lifetime. As such, we all have genius within us. Also, each of us has an area in life that is going to be a challenge. This could be family, health, financial, career or some other area. Certainly, there may be times when it may be in the best interest of a child to be managed a bit in order to help them achieve their potential. But this is done from the standpoint of supporting them to get past a hurdle, not from our projections of the future. We have moved into a period of great unknown. We are writing our present and future on a daily basis. When we act from our projections, we are taking action based on our previous experiences and our old beliefs, both of which are irrelevant to an unknown future. They are ideal if we are trying to re-experience the past and old paradigms but nothing else.

What would be extremely helpful to all the new children is parenting through flow instead of structure. This is accomplished by you as a parent or a grandparent being willing to throw everything that you thought you knew about parenting out the window at any given moment and to take a completely different trajectory based on what is called for in any given moment (Michaels, 2014).

Stability is still going to be important for the new children. Being present in the moment does not change this in any way, but many of you may still see structure as synonymous with stability. So be patient with yourself.

Humanity has lived for a very long time through the patterns of Separation consciousness. We love habit and structure as much as we love comfort food, but in reality, it is just structure. The new consciousness, vibrations, the new Earth and the Quantum children need something innovative. They need a *"flow of family"* rather than a *"structure of family."*

I do not pretend that this will be easy for you. Breaking old habits can be extremely difficult and yet all I'm really asking you is to be present in the moment and live within whatever the moment requires, knowing it is okay. This will take some getting used to. With anything that is new, there will be some ups and downs. The problem is not that you can or cannot do this. The problem is it has never been modeled for you. You are some of the first to take this leap. Great Congratulations!

We live in a time of great change. Being flexible, open-minded and creative are the skills that each of us needs to cultivate. Perhaps you would like to hear there is one perfect technique that works in every situation, but there isn't one. You are going to have to be courageous and willing to move into an unknown arena. Letting go of the concept of *right or wrong, good or bad* will be very helpful to you because everything is based on perspective. Change the perspective around something and the belief that it is right or wrong also changes.

Our minds are like a computer. They access their data, which are its experiences and beliefs of the past, then project into the future the results that might happen. This served us well in the past. However, we live in a time frame when all the old structures are collapsing. The data your brain is accessing may or may not be relevant anymore. Your soul's information, however, always is and in order to access it, you will need to be present in the moment and centered in your heart. This is why learning this for yourself and teaching it to your children is important. Equally significant is the capability to quiet your mind. And for this, you and your children will need to learn how to meditate.

If every 8-year old in the world would be taught meditation, we would eliminate violence in the world in one generation.

Dalai Lama

There are many ways to accomplish that and a lot of wonderful materials on the internet to guide you. I, personally, have always enjoyed guided meditations. As a hypnotherapist, I love to use light and sound devices in conjunction with guided meditations. They can help even novices get into meditative brain wave states in less than five minutes. Two of my grandchildren began using my glasses when they were only nine years old. (More information about these glasses is included in the appendix.) Learning how to completely quiet your mind is a skill that takes time and practice. I would encourage you to take a class or two in this area. I definitely believe it would be beneficial.

As I mentioned earlier, every time you tune within for answers, you help to reestablish trust of your Soul and trust of Source. As a child learns how to do this, it can be incredibly freeing for you as a parent. There is no more need for control. Interestingly, though, if you do not learn this skill for yourself, you won't be able to naturally trust your children regardless of the level they might reach. Just as you can love another only to the degree that you love yourself, you can only trust another to the extent that you trust yourself.

Conditioning the Limits

A lot has changed in society and consciousness over the last seventy five years. In the past, many cultures had the belief that negative reinforcement was the way to raise strong, tough children. *Spare the rod and spoil the child.* Discipline was the name of the game. If you were positive, then you were considered soft. As a consequence, we had the drill sergeant fathers and dragon moms. Life was tough and if you weren't tough enough, you wouldn't succeed. Parenting was based on the concept of survival of the fittest in many households. Everything was push, push, push because that was how we would survive in this dog-eat-dog world.

Society today has gotten better but still maintains a lot of conditioning that looks to the negative first instead of the positive. In school, does the teacher mark every answer that a student gets correct? No, she marks the mistakes. At work, the things we do well are often taken for granted. After all, this is what we are being paid for, right? Whereas, if we make a mistake, we can get fired. We are conditioned by fear of failure and this creates problems. Our desire for control is a type of fear. The greater your fear, the more obsessive you will be in desiring control. Furthermore, I can assure you that there is no way you can be in the *flow with parenting* when you are attempting to be in control. You have to trust the moment and just go with it.

We all would like our children to be happy and have a positive outlook on life. We want them to love themselves and have good self-esteem. We would like them to be brave and go through life without fear of failure. And finally, we would like our children to feel they could accomplish anything; that they have no limits. It sounds great, doesn't it? And yet one study at UCLA not all that long ago said the average one year old hears the word "*no*" four hundred times in a day. That is one hundred forty six thousand times a toddler would hear the word "*no*" between his or her first and second birthday. All too frequently, parents are focused on *what not to do* instead of *what to do*. Considering the fact that what you focus on expands and that everything you say and do around a child is absorbed directly into their subconscious, is it any wonder as a society we have failed in helping individuals have all these wonderful traits?

I realize that you would like your one year-old to see his or her second birthday. However, there has to be a better way of taking care of our children without saying the word "no" all the time. Generation after generation has conditioned their children by focusing on what they don't want to have occur. And then later in life, we ask them what they do want and they literally can't respond. One technique that you can use with the young children is to redirect them. Find something safe for them to do and distract them from what you would previously have said *no* to. In this way, you are actually saying *yes* instead of *no*.

Mothers with children who are two, three and four have an equal challenge. These children want to explore everything. This is what they are supposed to do. Our job as parents or grandparents is to keep them safe and to teach them about the physical reality that we live in. We want to teach them an awareness of the different dangers that exist around them. You can warn a child not to touch a hot stove all day long but at some point, the child is going to touch it. There is just something within us that still has to experience it. Parents with a swimming pool in their yard teach their children how to swim at the earliest age possible. Why? Because at some point the little ones are going to get in the pool by themselves.

We are constantly teaching and conditioning our fears. The more we are aware of this and catch ourselves, the better. You might think everyone would agree on what might be dangerous but this is not true. Horse cultures like the Plains Indian tribes, ranchers and farmers grew up on horses and consequently didn't fear having their children riding at the earliest ages possible. My wife and I live in Colorado and we have seen children that could hardly walk having fun skiing. Children who live in a fishing culture learn everything about the sea and being on a boat at very young ages. I have been flying airplanes for more than forty years and I have pictures of my son on my lap when he was only two while flying a light airplane. I remember seeing pictures of Evel Knievel, the stunt performer and daredevil motorcyclist, on a motorcycle at an extremely young age. All of us have things that we are comfortable with and know. We have no fears in these areas, but other areas that are unknown to us give us a different reaction.

We teach limits all the time and don't even realize it. Pay attention to your wordings. Is what you are saying carrying a subtle form of limitation? Certainly, telling a child *no* all the time creates limits, but what about the other words that we use such as *can't* and *don't*.

Could you still do your job as a parent if those three words were taken out of your vocabulary? It would be fun to see what you would come up with.

Positive Psychology

I am a firm believer in positive psychology and there are some very useful thoughts that have come up in this area. What the psychologists have found is we perform better in every area when done in a positive environment. No shock there. People love positive encouragement and recognition, yet most people in our society are conditioned to use these only as a reward for achieving something, not as the engine that drives the performance. We do our best work when we are happy first.

This was found to be true in virtually any group scenario. Groups and individuals who had positive leadership or a positive environment consistently outperformed the groups where their leaders or the environment were either negative or neutral. This included even the military, where the concept of having a tough commander is how it should be. Units with commanders who were openly encouraging were far more likely to win awards for efficiency and preparedness than those whose commanders displayed what we think of as the harsh "military taskmaster" style of leadership. (Achor, 2010)

Psychologist and business consultant, Marcial Losada, spent ten years studying the ratio of positive to negative interactions that would make a corporate team successful. Now, we know that a family is different from a corporate team, but I believe the premise of his research is also beneficial in the family group dynamic. What Losada found from his extensive mathematical modeling, was that a ratio of 2.9013 positive to negative interactions was necessary to make a corporate team successful. This meant that it took about three positive comments, experiences, or expressions to fend off the weakening effect of one negative one. This became known as the Losada line. Drop below it and supposedly your business would suffer. Operate above it and your group's performance would improve extensively, with the optimum effect occurring at a six to one ratio.

You as a parent or grandparent have the added benefits of being able to express love openly. A pat on the back, a loving caress, a gentle smile, and of course lots of hugs and kisses are all expressions available to you that aren't available in the workplace. And don't ever underestimate the power of your voice. What you say and how you say it can have effects that last a lifetime.

Growth Mindset vs. a Fixed Mindset

Generations past mine have done a much better job of being positive in order to create positive self-esteem among their children. This is great, but as with any concept that we think is perfect, there are nuances we don't take into account. All too often children who heard how good they were, weren't turning out as wonderful as the parents had intended. Part of it was the creation of an inflated ego, which was just the extreme opposite of a poor self-image, but this is only part of the story. What the psychologists found was this the children were developing what Carol Dweck, PhD (author of *Mindset: The Psychology of Success*) calls a **fixed mindset**. (Dweck, n.d.)

You see, the brains of the children were acting much like a computer. Computers work on a binary code of ones and zeros. Whatever pattern the parents were praising was either seen as on or off. Let's say, for example, that the child was told consistently that he or she was *smart*. As the child's brain accepted the thought of being *smart*, it also created within it the programming of the alternate of smart or *not smart*. This is the part that was unseen. Let's assume these children actually were quite bright and consequently breezed through the early school years. Eventually, however, they hit an area of difficulty, normally around middle school, and then the mess began. They would now be faced with the other side of the program that was the *not smart* portion. The children's minds weren't

194

embracing the challenge; they weren't seeing themselves as smart anymore. They were seeing themselves as not smart and shutting down. This didn't happen in every instance but it did happen frequently. These children were going through an identity crisis and they didn't know how to handle it.

A **growth** mindset, on the contrary, embraces the challenge, and success is not measured by whether you won or lost but by your learning and growing. In this case, when children hit a bump in the road, they aren't stymied by a challenge. They are enlivened. In both instances, the parents are offering positive encouragement, but where the difference lies is what they are emphasizing. A growth mindset is focused on celebrating the learning and growth that is going on, a celebration of winning or the completion of an exercise being secondary. Dr. Dweck has a program she developed called *"Brainology"* on her website (www.mindsetworks.com) where she teaches students about the plasticity of the brain and how it grows. Our minds love it when they can assign a meaning to a particular activity. A child could then begin to imagine his or her brain expanding when taking on a challenging problem instead of shutting down, as was the case with the individuals that had developed a fixed mindset.

How you praise and the types of praise develop these two different mindsets. When you are focused on a growth mindset, your questions naturally are around what they might have learned and your enthusiasm is about their growth. You might even be especially congratulatory when they hit a challenge and are able to work through it. It just becomes a different point of focus from the more common one of *did you win or lose*? The very best athletic coaches use the growth mindset philosophy because there will always be wins and losses. To them, their point of focus is, *did we, as a team, get better than we were yesterday?*

Two Practices

There are two practices I would like to offer that would help you create a different perspective in your life to counteract all the negative conditioning we are bombarded with daily.

The first is an exercise recommended in Esther Hicks's *Ask and it is Given* (Hicks, 2004). Most of society has been conditioned to see a problem area in individuals they come in contact with. They are drawn to see what they don't like about someone instead of what they do like. This exercise is designed to switch this around. So regardless how loving or despicable someone might be, your job would be to take a few moments each day to write in a journal the positive attributes of several individuals. You could, of course, start with your family and then as you get more practice expand into other people in your life.

A great deal of the human experience is learning about *love*. Ideally, we would like to go through our days having only loving thoughts but unfortunately, this is a challenge for most of us. Exercises like this help to turn that around. So to begin this practice write down things that you love and like about the people you are close to. Then when you are more comfortable, challenge yourself to find things you like and love about those whose beliefs are different from yours. Have fun with it.

The second practice is from Shawn Achor's *The Happiness Advantage* (Achor, 2010). It is very similar to the first one but its focus is on happiness. What you do is share with your family or friends over dinner three things that made you smile or brought you joy over the last twenty four hours. Each day you come up with three new events or incidences. You weren't to use the same ones twice. This gets your brain radar focused on finding joy, happiness, beauty and love around you all day.

Have fun with these and see where they may take you.

Points to Remember

1. Children will always need our nurturing and support. That is always going to be important, but the managing aspect of parenting needs to be diminished greatly.

2. What would be extremely helpful to all the new children is parenting through flow instead of structure. This is accomplished by you as a parent or a grandparent being willing to throw everything that you thought you knew about parenting out the window at any given moment and to take a completely different trajectory based on what is called for in any given moment.

3. The Quantum children need a *"flow of family"* rather than a *"structure of family."*

4. We do our best work when we are happy first.

5. The optimum ratio of positive expressions to negative is 6 to 1.

6. When you focus on growth and learning you create a growth mindset within a child. This mindset helps children embrace challenges when they occur.

14

Conclusion

When I write, I begin by connecting my intuitive-self to the group consciousness of the Quantum children and the Councils of Light who look over them. This is where Mother Mary and the Order of Isis come in. The Order of Isis is sometimes referred to as the Order of the Magdalene, so as you can imagine, Jeshua and Mary Magdalene's energy is an important part of this book as well. My job is to listen, write and to blend the information as seamlessly as I can. Hopefully, I have done a good job with this.

It has been a true pleasure working with Mother Mary and the Order of Isis in the writing of this book. There is so much information they wish to convey that a single book could ever do it justice, so Book 2 in this series is already in the making.

So far, we have been able to cover some of the history of the shift in consciousness that is taking place and how the Quantum children fit in. In general, the Quantum children are aligned for fourth density consciousness and any of the patterns of third density are not going to work well with them. The problem, of course, is they are arriving into a world that is still dominated by Separation consciousness and other third density paradigms.

The structures of our world are slow to change. Whether it is power, politics or money keeping them in place doesn't matter. They do not support the Quantum children and we, as parents and grandparents, need to make different choices. Politics, religion, education, and the medical community are all aspects of our society that each of us is connected to in various ways. Certainly, different pieces of these structures are still beneficial to society, but a great portion of them is not. Unfortunately, when we connect with a structure we tend to accept all of it and don't separate the wheat from the chaff. This is due to our conditioning. We are bombarded daily by these structures with images that convey the thoughts and beliefs of those in control. It is only by disconnecting from this conditioning that we can begin to see different perspectives and consequently make different choices.

We are moving into a reality that is unknown to many of us and change can be scary. We tend to stay with the current structures, not because of the benefit they provide for us but because they are what we know. This is the same level of thought that keeps an individual in an abusive marriage. When you are disconnected from the situation, it is easy to see it for what it is. When you have an emotional attachment to the situation or structure it certainly is more difficult to break away.

Up to now we have focused a lot of our attention on being healthy and happy. All of the points that we've looked at are important, but let me share with you my core beliefs in this area.

- ➢ You are a divine creator being, but do you act from that fact?
  - o Pay your gratitude forward and then flow with the experiences that the universe brings to you.
- ➢ See your children in their highest light.
- ➢ What are you mirroring for your children?
- ➢ Own your health. Take back your power and tune within for your choices.
- ➢ Reestablish your trust of self
- ➢ Watch the Dosage.
- ➢ We are vibrational creatures living in a vibrational universe. As such energy and informational medicine represent the future of medicine.
- ➢ Each of us has to be more discerning and more proactive than ever before in the area of health for your family.
- ➢ Play with the practices of positive psychology and see how they can create a difference within your family.

Two of my favorite sayings or thoughts are…

> ➢ I choose the path of joy

And when things go a bit sideways

> ➢ How can it get any better than this?

The Quantum children are very sensitive and the overriding message given to me was *watch the dosage*. I had a chance recently to talk to a doctor that I was paired with on a casual round of golf. We had never met before. During the play, I had a chance to ask him what his reaction would be if a parent conveyed to him that their child was sensitive and if he would take that into consideration. His response was "how does she know?" In essence, what he was saying to me was he believes only sources that are part of his medical structure. This is a problem all of us are going to have to be creative to get around because I don't believe his mindset is a unique one in the medical field. They have their way of doing things and your input as a parent is not being valued as it should be.

The medical community has been given an enormous amount of empirical data from parents when their children have been harmed by vaccines. Instead of taking action, they deny the existence of a problem. I know these children are not victims, but this still does not keep my heart from crying out when I see children harmed unnecessarily by a system that doesn't want to change.

I consider energy and informational medicine to be our future. Unfortunately, those who control the structures of medicine, the American Medical Association, the Food and Drug Administration, and the Center for Disease Control are a hundred years behind holistic medicine in this area. I introduced these fields of study to you because I believe they can be a great benefit to you and your family. You need better options and as we all know, allopathic medicine limits itself to only two: surgery or drugs.

Our days of parenting like Mom and Dad are over. We are entering into a whole new world and I know you will do the very best you can. The most poignant thing I can offer to you is this...

Be willing, in any given moment, to completely disregard everything you know about parenting and take a different tack, just because that is what is called for in the moment.

Book 2

Do I know all that is to be included in Book 2? No, just as in Book 1, I was getting new information all the time I was writing and I expect the same thing to occur for this next installment. I certainly have enough material to fill up several books right now but my job is not to control the material. My job is to be open and listen. As I flow with the inspirations that come to me, the book takes shape. So I will merely get started and then see where the energy takes me.

There are a lot of areas I haven't touched on yet. Education and nutrition are certainly two very important topics that I wish to explore. Also, there are understandings on how we can clear some of our old and outdated beliefs. For this, we'll perhaps explore Access Consciousness and Ho'oponopono. Competition is considered wonderful and necessary in this world but it is cooperation that has a much higher vibration. Many people see goal-setting as imperative to achievement, and yet within my understandings of how we manifest in the physical world there are at least two levels above that. From this perspective, goal-setting is basically high school-level material. I would like to explore some of the next levels of understandings with you. And then we have images of what the new world will look like, all of which will take us into the unknown.

I spent more than a decade working with Lesley Michaels and her channeled material from Jeshua and Mary. Three years of that were spent in an intensive course they called "The Apprenticeship to Awakening Divinity." I would also like to share with you understandings from those teachings.

Most importantly, before I leave you, I want to thank you for being here and helping all of humanity shift into its next stage of evolution. My understanding is this is the largest shift in consciousness to ever be undertaken on this planet and you are a very important piece of this puzzle.

Thank you for choosing to be here at this time.

Thank you for being you.

Section 5

Points to Remember

Points to Remember

1. Changing Paradigms

1. We are at the end of a great cycle.

2. The paradigms and structures of fear, judgment and competition do not serve the new children.

3. For a parent or grandparent, it is important to remember we are constantly modeling for our children.

4. These children are like a brand-new computer, and the programs of the past are not in alignment with their consciousness.

5. The conditioning of our children goes all the way back to the point of conception.

6. Everything is energy.

7. We are vibrational creatures living in a vibrational universe.

8. We are far more than just our physical body.

9. Life is not a single lifetime, it is a continuum, and as an unlimited soul, we can choose from an infinite number of choices the experiences that we wish to have.

2. Mankind is Constantly Evolving

1. Mankind is constantly evolving.

2. The term **density** is used because it is a specific vibratory rate and level of consciousness.

3. These Quantum children are providing us with an example of where we are moving to, and we have a great opportunity to model them as we move through our own shifts.

4. Each group has their own purpose.

5. The purpose of the Quantum children is – to teach humanity to stop Doing life and to start Living life.

6. Help the new children to find joy and happiness and to live it with great enthusiasm.

7. The Quantum children are aligned with Unity consciousness. Belief structures based in Separation will act like a computer virus within them.

3. Zack's Story

1. Connect with your son or daughter through every phase of the pregnancy.

2. Did you notice how Anne worked with little Zack more as a soul than as a little baby?

3. Even when he was a one and a half pound baby, Anne knew that Zack was guiding his medical care.

4. Anne and Tom did the best that they could working through the structure of the established medical situation, keeping things positive and not allowing the structure to dictate to them.

5. Anne and Tom have from the beginning recognized that Zack's needs were different and that many of the things offered by the medical or education communities would not work for him.

6. **Zack came into this world to live his own life and Anne and Tom trusted him.**

4. Creating our Reality

1. When we live from the understanding that we are the creators of our reality, the archetype of victimhood then is allowed to heal.

2. The current circumstances in your life are only a ten percent indicator of your happiness.

3. We are vibrational beings living in a vibrational universe.

4. We are shifting from **doing** to **being**.

5. What you focus on expands.

6. In 2012, we as a collective removed our largest veil that was slowing down our manifestations. We are now creating our positive thoughts and our fear one hundred times faster than before.

7. You must become that which you desire to attract to yourself.

8. Seventeen seconds of pure thought is the equivalent of two thousand action hours. Sixty eight seconds of pure thought equates to two million.

9. Whether something is good, bad, right or wrong is always based on a perspective and a judgment.

5. Gratitude

1. That which your mind can conceive and believe you can achieve.

2. Virtually every creation that you have ever wanted, ever desired on any level, already exists for you within the time continuum.

3. As we share gratitude forward, we begin to stabilize ourselves in the absolute awareness that everything we experience was and is chosen.

4. Choices must be made and actions taken, but if you aren't in a state of receivership and allowing, nothing will come to pass.

5. Gratitude places each of us in our greatest position of receptivity.

6. The Art of Worry

1. Worrying is actually a fear of a possible future outcome that we project towards our children. We are putting our energy into exactly what we don't want to have happen.

2. When it comes to manifesting and thoughts, the universe is all inclusive. It doesn't see the word or concept of "not," "no,"

or "I don't want ..." It only sees where you're putting your energy.

3. Ideally, you could see your children as amazing divine creators, present in the moment and following their hearts. Their life path flowing before them effortlessly. (The Pygmalion Effect)

4. Do you **know** in your heart that your child has genius within them or do you just **think** it?

5. You are one hundred percent human **and** one hundred percent divine.

6. Our connection with, and effect on our children happen long before they are born.

7. The child chooses you, the parent, based on all of the potentials available that you can provide.

7. Healthy and Happy

1. "I'll be happy when..." is backward to how the universe works.

2. Adopt the five/ten approach.

3. I **choose** the path of Joy.

4. *How can it get any better than this?*

5. When you tune within you are healing aspects of your **trust of yourself** and **trust of your soul**.

6. Each and every time you activate internal communication between your human self and soul self, you express trust in both, by simply offering room for mutual self-expression.

8. An Interesting Point of View

1. The current model is based on the point of view that sees the physical body like a machine. (Newtonian physics)

2. At any one point in time, both quantum and Newtonian points of view might be correct.

3. Germ theory is victimhood consciousness. The care of the Terrain of the body is based in Quantum understandings.

4. **Watch the Dosage.**

5. Dr. McBride's point of view is that vaccines were designed for healthier immune systems than what our children have today and that no child should be given any type of vaccine unless you test their intestinal flora first.

6. Dr. McBride also recommends that no vaccines should be administered before the age of three.

9. Synthetics and Antibiotics

1. Currently, there are more than eighty thousand chemicals that the FDA considers legal that we are exposed to all the time.

2. To use a Synthetic anything is an insult to the body.

3. Genetic modification is the process of forcing genes from one species into another entirely unrelated species.

4. Because antibiotics are so accepted, in many ways they are even more dangerous than GMOs to your health.

5. Eighty percent of your immune function originates with your intestinal flora.

10. Body and Soul Speak

1. When you address a problem from only the physical side of things it is the equivalent of *cutting off the top of a weed, leaving its roots alone, allowing it to grow back at a later time.*

2. Your higher levels of consciousness are speaking to you through your body.

3. Certainly, one of the most important pieces of information you can provide for yourself is where you are out of balance in your life.

4. Your physical body was set up so that it would reflect back to you everything that is going on in your life.

5. The code that is used is fairly simple once you know what to look for. The simplest place to start is to think of what any particular body part does for the body.

11. Informational Fields of the Body

1. The current medical model is not one of Wellness; unfortunately, it is one that simply manages illness.

2. To the medical community, your consciousness has no effect on what is going on in the body. Physical cause and effect are its primary focus.

3. Morphogenetic fields are fields of information that regulate and determine how different genes will be combined, as well as which genes will be switched on or off in our bodies.

4. Many of the instantaneous healings we have had over the millenniums are a result of radical and sudden changes in an individual's information field.

5. One of the ways of looking at disease is as scrambled or disrupted information that is being provided to the body. Another term for this is incoherent information. Fix the incoherence and the body will respond accordingly.

12. Imprints and Homeopathy

1. For decades, we all have been exposed to synthetic products that have a hugely detrimental effect on our health. The sensitivities of the new children magnify exponentially the negative effects of these products.

2. Cells are one hundred times more receptive to energy and information than they are to chemicals

3. Homeopathy is a quantum medical system based on the concept that like cures like.

4. Homeopathy, more than any other modality, has been fought by the allopathic community, not because it's a poor treatment, but rather, a very beneficial one, and therefore seen as its greatest competitor.

5. Everything is energy. Everything has a vibration and a frequency, and as our vibration gets higher, as is the case for the Quantum children, it is much easier for us to help them using vibrational and informational medicine versus the synthetics of the drug industry.

6. The most important thing you need to do in regard to your health and that of your child's is to **_OWN IT_**.

13. Father Knows Best

1. Children will always need our nurturing and support. That is always going to be important, but the managing aspect of parenting needs to be diminished greatly.

2. What would be extremely helpful to all the new children is parenting through flow instead of structure. This is accomplished by you as a parent or a grandparent being willing to throw everything that you thought you knew about parenting out the window at any given moment and to take a completely different trajectory based on what is called for in any given moment.

3. The Quantum children need a "*flow of family*" rather than a "*structure of family.*"

4. We do our best work when we are happy first.

5. The optimum ratio of positive expressions to negative is six to one.

6. When you focus on growth and learning you create a growth mindset within a child. This mindset helps children embrace challenges when they occur.

Section 6

References

Recommended Books

Shawn Achor

- The Happiness Advantage

Dr. Natasha Campbell-McBride

- GAPS: Gut and Psychology Syndrome

Dolores Cannon

- The Convoluted Universe Series
- The Three Waves of Volunteers and the New Earth

Julia Cannon

- Soul Speak: The Language of Your Body

John R. Christopher

- School of Natural Healing

Dr. Joe Dispenza

- Breaking the Habit of Being Yourself
- You are the Placebo
- Evolve your Brain, The Science of Changing Your Mind

Esther and Jerry Hicks

- The Law of Attraction
- Ask and It is Given
- The Astonishing Power Of Emotions
- The Vortex

Life Science Publishing

- Essential Oils desk reference

Dr. Bruce Lipton

- The Biology of Belief
- Spontaneous Evolution

Meg Blackburn Losey

- The Children of Now
- Parenting the Children of Now: Practicing Health, Spirit, and Awareness to Transcend Generations

Jenny McCarthy

- Louder than Words: A Mother's Journey to Heal Autism

Lynne Mc Taggart

- The Field
- What Doctors Don't Tell You

Lesley Michaels

- Just Roll Over and Float

Patrick Porter PhD

- Discover the Language of the Mind
- Awaken the Genius

Ken Robinson

- The Element
- Out of Our Minds
- Finding Your Element

Aviva Jill Romm

- Babies and Children: A Commonsense Naturally Healthy Guide to Herbal Remedies, Nutrition, and Health

Dr. Rupert Sheldrake

- Science Set Free: 10 Paths to New Discovery
- Morphic Resonance: The Nature of Formative Causation

Dr. Jerry Tennant, MD

- Healing is Voltage: Acupuncture Muscle Batteries

Eckhart Tolle

- The Power of Now

Cheryl Townsley

- Kid Smart: Raising a Healthy Child

Dana Ullman

- Homeopath: Medicine for the 21st Century

David Wilcock

- The Source Field Investigations
- The Synchronicity Key
- The Ascension Mysteries

Websites and Newsletters

www.Gaia.com

This website hosts some of the best information available to you. It contains more than five thousand different titles on every holistic subject imaginable and it is only ten dollars a month. Here are three of my favorites

David Wilcock has two series that are a must-see:

- Cosmic Disclosure
- Wisdom Teachings

Regina Meredith

Regina is one of the best interviewers you will ever find. She has hundreds of interviews on every topic you can imagine in the holistic field.

Dolores Cannon

www.dolorescannon.com/

Dr. Mercola

www.mercola.com

(Great newsletter on all forms of health topics)

Lynne McTaggert

www.lynnemctaggart.com

What Doctors Don't Tell You newsletter

Kimberly and Foster Gamble

www.Thrivemovement.com

Dr. Sherri Tenpenny

www.drtenpenny.com

(education about vaccines)

The Natural News

www.naturalnew.com

Dr. Rupert Sheldrake

www.sheldrake.org/

Dr. Joe Dispenza

http://www.drjoedispenza.com/

Esther and Jerry Hicks

http://www.abraham-hicks.com/

Movies and TED Talks

Movies

The Secret

What the Bleep do We Know

Thrive

The Living Matrix

VAXXED: From Cover-up to Catastrophe

Water the Great Mystery

Michael Moore's

- Where to Invade Next
- Sicko

TED Talks

Logan LaPlante…Hackschooling

Sir Ken Robinson…Do Schools Kill Creativity

Simon Sinek (Sept 2009)

Rupert Sheldrake (his talk can be found on YouTube)

Shawn Achor, The happy secret to better work

Appendices

Appendix 1 - A Special Interview with Dr. Natasha Campbell-McBride
> By Dr. Mercola on Autism

Appendix 2 - Interview with Gisela Hoffman

Appendix 3 - Meditation and the Braintap Glasses

Appendix 4 - A short explanation about different modalities within Alternative and Natural Medicine

> ➢ Essential Oils
> ➢ Acupuncture
> ➢ Energy Medicine
> ➢ Nutritional Health and Healing

Appendix 5 - Kinesiology

Appendix 1

A Special Interview with
Dr. Natasha Campbell-McBride

By Dr. Mercola

http://articles.mercola.com/sites/articles/archive/2012/05/12/dr-campbell-mcbride-on-gaps.aspx

(Mercola, Fermented Foods Contain 100 TIMES More Probiotics than a Supplement, 2012)

This is a wonderful interview by Dr. Mercola on autism. I am including only the first portion so that you have an idea of exactly how powerful this information is. You can download the full transcript from Dr. Mercola's website as well and see the video of the interview if you would prefer.

DM: Dr. Joseph Mercola
DC: Dr. Natasha Campbell-McBride

Introduction:

DM: Welcome, everyone. This is Dr. Mercola. I'm here today with Dr. Natasha Campbell-McBride, who is going to enlighten us about an interesting topic, which is gut and psychology syndrome. It really is a natural treatment for autism, ADHD, dyslexia, dyspraxia, depression and schizophrenia.

Welcome, Dr. Campbell.

DC: Thank you. I'm delighted to be here.

DM: We're delighted to have you. Could you tell me a little bit about what your training is, clinically and academically, and how you acquired your expertise in this area?

DC: I'm a medical doctor. I got my first postgraduate degree when I was a young doctor in neurology. I worked as a neurologist and a neurosurgeon for several years. Then I started my family.

My first-born son was diagnosed autistic at the age of three, which threw me into a huge learning curve, because I had to find a solution to his problem because my own profession had nothing to offer, which was a bit of a shock for me.

Having found all those solutions, I went back to the university. I completed a second postgraduate degree in human nutrition and learned many more other things. As a result, my son fully recovered. He is not autistic anymore. He is living a normal life.

I have a clinic in Cambridge in England, in the UK, which is very busy with children and adults with learning disabilities, neurological disorders, psychiatric disorders, and children and adults with immune disorders and digestive problems.

DM: What country did you receive your medical training in?

DC: I'm Russian. I was trained as a doctor in Russia. I practiced as a doctor, as a neurologist, in Russia. Then I started my family and moved to the UK. So the whole disaster with my first child happened in the UK.

DM: Was your child born in the UK?

DC: Yes. He was born in the UK. Now I have lived in the UK for the last twenty years and have practiced there.

DM: How long did it take you to acquire the expertise and understanding to be able to nurture your child through the autism challenge and back into a normal functioning child?

DC: Well, many parents understood and I understood the same thing: that children are given to us to teach us lessons. The learning curve is very fast and very steep; usually particularly with a child with autism, because the younger the child is when you start the treatment, the better the results are. The longer you let the child sit in

221

that autistic form, the more difficult it is to pull them out of it and the less impressive the results are.

When we started the treatment, the GAPS treatment I'm talking about now, at the age of two, three, four up to five, you give your child a real chance to completely recover from autism, from ADHD, from ADD, and dyslexia and dyspraxia, and that larger group of children who do not fit into any diagnostic box.

They may have a little bit of autism and a little bit of ADHD and a little bit of dyslexia and a little bit of dyspraxia and a little bit of something else, but none of it is conclusive enough to fit that child into a diagnostic box.

These are the children with whom doctors usually procrastinate. They ask the parents to bring the child in six months and again in six months to observe the child in order to just give the child a diagnosis and very precious, very valuable time gets wasted that way while the child could have been helped.

DM: When did you graduate medical school? What year?

DC: I graduated in 1984.

DM: So about the same time I did. Do you recall the incidence of autism around then? Was it about one in a hundred thousand or so? What is your current estimate as to the incidence today in the UK?

DC: It was one in ten thousand when I graduated. It was a very rare disorder. Even I, as a medical graduate, had never seen an autistic patient. By the time I graduated from my medical school I had never seen an autistic individual. I have seen other psychiatric conditions through my course in psychiatry but had never seen an autistic child. To be honest, the first autistic child that I had encountered was my own.

As I said, twenty years ago in the Western world — and certainly in the English-speaking world — we were diagnosing one child in ten thousand. Five years ago we were diagnosing one child in a hundred and fifty which is almost a forty fold increase in incidence. Now in Britain and some countries, we are diagnosing one child in sixty six.

As I understand that, the numbers are similar in some states in America, in some areas of the states in America; the same in Australia and the same in New Zealand.

I have just come back from Hungary; the incidence there is not as high, but it is getting close to one child in a hundred and fifty.

DM: That's a dramatic increase. Basically a fifty fold increase from the time you and I started practicing. Have you come to any conclusions as to what you understand your beliefs are as to what are the primary contributing factors to this dramatic increase?

DC: Absolutely, I have no doubt whatsoever that these children are born with a perfectly normal brain and perfectly normal sensory organs and they are supposed to function normally. What happens to these children – and that's my absolute belief – and that's what GAPS (Gut and Psychology Syndrome) describes. The very name establishes a connection between the functioning of the digestive system and the functioning of the brain.

What happens in these children is they develop an abnormal gut flora from the beginning of their lives. As a result, their digestive system instead of being a source of nourishment for these children becomes a major source of toxicity. These pathogenic microbes inside their digestive tract damage the integrity of the gut wall.

So all sort of toxins and microbes flood into the bloodstream of the child and get into the brain of the child. That usually happens in the second year of life in children who were breastfed because breastfeeding provides a protection against this abnormal gut flora. In children who were not breastfed, I see the symptoms of autism developing in the first year of life. So breastfeeding is crucial to protect these children.

Dr. Mercola interviewed Dr. Campbell-McBride for about an hour, so the full transcription is about twenty pages long, which is why I chose to only give you an introduction to this material.

Appendix 2

Interview with Gisela Hoffman

I had a chance to interview Gisela Hoffman when I was doing some of my research for this book. Gisela is the daughter of Hanna Kroeger.

Hanna Kroeger was one of the foremost authorities on herbs, homeopathic remedies and natural healing techniques in the country. In 1999, she was named one of the six outstanding holistic pioneers of the twentieth century along with Dr. Edward Bach, Edgar Cayce, Dr. John Christopher, Linus Pauling and Ann Wigmore. She spent her entire life developing natural herbal and homeopathic remedies at her educational center, Peaceful Meadow Retreat, in Boulder, Colorado. During her lifetime, Hanna trained, healed and inspired thousands of people and wrote twenty books that contain information about the uses for her unique herbal combinations and Vibropathic™ remedies. She also created one of this country's first health food stores in 1956.

Gisela Hoffman took over her mother's work when Hanna passed away in 1998. Gisela was a college statistics professor for many years, followed by a career in designing databases for several prominent insurance companies. She finds that her third career as Minister of the Chapel of Miracles, Intuitive Counselor in physical and spiritual matters and teacher at the Peaceful Meadow Retreat in Colorado, is by far the most satisfying and rewarding one. She lectures across the country and has dedicated her life to helping her fellow human beings live their lives fully through natural healing techniques.

Here are some excerpts and notes from my interview with her.

MO — is myself (Michael)
GH — is Gisela's responses

MO: Do you have a favorite book on natural healing?

GH: One book that I would definitely recommend was a book by John Christopher. He was one of the twentieth century's greatest herbalists and he wrote a book for parents on natural healing methods for children. (It is in the reference section). It was a step-by-step answer to many different problems. As an example, if a child has colic, why don't you try this? That type of thing.

MO: What advice do you have for the readers?

GH: One of the primary things I would put in your book is that, and you hinted at it, is that the toxins—the vaccinations and drugs that they are giving the children are suppressing their immune system, and the consequences, the immediate result is that they will have fewer symptoms, but the long-term results will be much different.

GH: When there are chronic problems or constantly reoccurring problems, the parents need to take a strong look at the food they are giving the child. If it is an occasional problem I would look at flower essences or other homeopathics, but if it is chronic look at the food.

MO: Could you explain flower essences a little more?

GH: The flower essence Chamomilla, as an example, will immediately take a child out of a state of fussiness. Say, for example, that a child is teething and you are in a grocery store and he begins to throw a temper tantrum. Even if you give them what they want they still won't stop. A flower essence like Chamomilla will cut off the tantrum. You can just spray a little of the essence in their face. That is all that it takes and it will cut it out almost instantly.

MO: We know homeopathic remedies work. Do you know how?

GH: They really don't know. I do believe that Bruce Lipton came extremely close, though. In his latest book, he described how a cell would have its protein antennas out, and they would shrink from any toxin that they came in contact with and that would open up to an energy. In other words, it will pick up vitamin C in its natural form, or an energetic version, but it will shy away from any unnatural form.

MO: How would homeopathic remedies have been made back in the 1800s?

GH: They would have been done much the way they are now. Take diphtheria, for example. A sample of tissue would be taken from a diphtheria child. All it would take is a little bit of mucus, and then just as now, it would be diluted in a solution over and over until only the essence of diphtheria remained. The dose would then be given to the child, triggering the healing response.

MO: Are there homeopathics for every vaccine on the market?

GH: Yes.

MO: How would a homeopathic affect the informational hologram?

GH: That is exactly what it does. It works with the non-physical body, the vibration, the holographic image of the body, and it helps the body in some way to become unstuck. In other words, the body is stuck when it is in disease mode and the homeopathic unsticks it. Once the body becomes unstuck, a type of domino effect then occurs as the body opens up to its natural healing response.

MO: The diluted homeopathic, you said that it was actually more powerful the more diluted it was.

GH: Yes.

MO: Please expand upon that for me.

227

GH: What happens on a homeopathic, if you have less dilution it hits the physical body, the more diluted…it hits the spiritual body. For example, the postman who had the severe depression. This is a spiritual-emotional symptom that is beyond the body, even though it was in the body. In order to hit it you have to have very etheric; namely, dilute the homeopathic many times over and you will hit the etheric-level energy. Which will then filter down into the physical energy. If you take something like a homeopathic for worms, you don't want it diluted that much. In other words, a six to twenty times dilution will hit the physical manifestation better. If you have a very depressed child or autistic child, you will need the higher dosage because their emotions and spirits are the primary problems. The dose has to go there first before you can get the immune system to heal the body. So in other words, the blueprint has to be healed first.

MO: Take me through how you would approach the healing of a young child that has become autistic, from a homeopathic point of view.

GH: As a homeopath, first, I would go after the actual viruses or the energy of the viruses that were planted in his body. The measles, mumps and rubella as an example. So you need a very diluted homeopathic to get rid of the measles, mumps and rubella virus energy impression. Then you'd need something to rebuild the brain energy; namely, the mercury homeopathic. I would look at a mercury homeopathic anywhere between 6X or C? and 30C dilution. So we would want to get rid of the mercury, get rid of the formaldehyde, and get rid of any other things that might have been injected with the MMR.

The reason the MMR is so dangerous is because it has all of these substances besides the virus. If they would give them simple measles vaccine without the formaldehyde and mercury in it, in other words, single-dose, it would be less of a problem. Single-dose versions should not need mercury to kill the bacteria. I believe that is used primarily in the multi-vial shots.

Single-vial vaccine only is what you want.

So, now the medical practitioners are hitting twenty people per vial. The last person on that vial – or the bottom people – get a heck of a lot more mercury or other heavy metals than the first ones. The vial is supposed to be shaken in between uses but you are still going to get more of the heavy metals there at the end.

I know a friend of mine whose daughter got very ill and if I remember correctly, the whole family had to be vaccinated because they were being sent to Saudi Arabia. The doctor was using the same vial and vaccinating each one of them from that vial. The little girl was last, and she evidently got a very heavy dose of the mercury and it caused her immense problems, many of them came out later. She had cancer. She was never well after that.

MO: In regard to the children being *sensitive,* how should one *watch the dosage?*

GH: Do not use vaccines that include two or more vaccines. Do not do DPT. Do not do MMR. Do them separately if you must vaccinate. Do diphtheria separately from whooping cough, from tetanus. So the child gets three shots rather than one. But the DPT shot and the MMR shots are way too much for the kids.

The shots are normally given according to the weight of the child and their additional sensitivities are not taken into consideration.

MO: That was the overall problem that I kept seeing in my meditations. The vibrational mass of these children is so much lighter than the children that the vaccines were initially designed for. As a consequence, the standard practice is overdosing the kids.

GH: Absolutely!

MO: In my meditations, I was consistently getting the message that if the child is to be vaccinated, it should be much later in his life – certainly not in the early years – and that is being reasonably accepted by the medical community. I believe many pediatricians are open to waiting until age two or three. What would you say about that?

GH: In one study that I saw, it was decided to try to give absolutely no shots to kids until after two years of age. They had zero Sudden Infant Death. The study has shown that the kids will do a lot better, that the counts of the antibodies are a lot better, if the kids don't get the vaccinations until later.

Fevers

GH: Kids, in general, need to have fevers. A fever is a good thing for a child until it gets to be one hundred and four or above. If the immune system is not allowed to have a fever, it will try for the rest of that child's life to have a fever to get rid of the toxins that are in the body.

MO: So is it a natural thing for the body to try to burn things off from time to time?

GH: Yes. Viruses and bacteria get burned off at a temperature between one hundred and three and one hundred and four. It is very natural.

MO: So, does the body of a young child need to develop its own ability to handle the bacteria, viruses and other organisms that it is naturally exposed to?

GH: Yes.

I remember one talk by a lady who said, "You know, at six weeks of age the baby will normally have some form of a rash on its body. And will have a slight fever. Frequently, the mother will get so fearful and will race the child to the doctor who will suppress that, frequently with antibiotics, which means that the immune system has lost a chance to stretch and test itself.

MO: It's like doing reps at the gym.

GH: Yes, that's right. And so when you give the children antibiotics to suppress that fever, it will come back in six weeks as a much greater fever and it will try again. At that point, it is usually much greater and will probably be dealing with all three: fungus, bacteria and viruses.

If they take antibiotics, they will only go after the bacteria but the fungus and the viruses have to be burned off. That is how the body heals them. But that's suppressed and cannot burn off with the antibiotics. And so the body's fever will go into a rest state and come again in about six weeks to try again. This cycle can continue until one day you are at a place where you cannot get an antibiotic. For example, let's say that he or she was away at college and couldn't get an antibiotic. They would have two weeks of hell where the body is extremely feverish with pain, burning off everything. At that point, the immune system will then be able to fight everything that comes into its domain.

MO: Do the body's temperature and thermal regulating system have to be developed?

GH: Yes. It is imperative and that would be a great thing to let people know. If that is suppressed in any way, the immune system just cannot work.

MO: It's interesting because when I was a child, we tended to let fevers run their course much more than people do today.

But then as our children have come along there has been more use of antibiotics; at least I know that was the case with my children. It's interesting how quickly we have been conditioned by the medical community too, just in case, go see the doctor. And then doctors, in general, have been conditioned to feel that they have to DO something, which often winds up with them writing a prescription. It is a circle that serves none. So let's say we had a set of parents that wish to detox their child from the vaccinations. What is on the market that would do that as a homeopathic remedy?

GH: There is the homeopathic Mercury.

231

MO: Is there something for Aluminum too?

GH: Yes, there is Homeopathic Alumina to get rid of the aluminum. There is also Chemex that will get rid of a whole lot of chemicals, like the formaldehyde that they put in there as well.

And then there is Thuja. It will help a lot.

MO: What is that?

GH: It is a homeopathic to neutralize excess virus activity in the immune system. Give the children Thuja every day, three days before the vaccination. After they have the vaccination, give them Thuja at least for a week, if not two weeks, to get rid of most of it. And if the child is old enough, have them suck on lemon drops and then spit them out. The excess residue will be transferred from the blood into the parotid glands and spit out.

MO: Do you really feel that a lot of women would both vaccinate and attempt to neutralize the vaccination at the same time?

GH: Absolutely. One of the problems that happens is if a woman refuses to vaccinate the kids, if they get divorced, the courts will give the kids to the husband. The judge could say you were not taking proper care of the kids. I've known women that have lost the children over this.

MO: Even if the husband was part of the same decision?

GH: Yes. He could conceivably use that against her unless they both signed an agreement. So if the marriage is shaky the mother has to consider this.

So an option is to take the Thuja, use the lemon drops and then after take another two weeks of Thuja. It will get rid of many of the problems.

MO: How can the parent push the pediatricians to do the vaccines much later?

GH: I've had quite a few people who have gotten empowered and they've said to the pediatrician, "I am not ready for this. Let us talk about it when the child is two years old." Many pediatricians are actually willing to go along. In the future, you could do the single dose if you still chose. The later you do it, the safer it is. The other thing is to really get mothers to be able to see that a fever is really a good thing. That we don't have to be scared of fevers.

MO: But our society has been conditioned to be scared of any kind of discomfort.

GH: Yes.

MO: You started early on in our conversation describing some basic things that the child would do to stretch its immune system: the rash at six weeks, and a light temperature. Carry that on, please. How about at age two or three?

GH: If you do not vaccinate the child, the child will have light temperature sessions, probably every six months to indicate that the immune system is working. A fever every year or six months is a good sign that the immune system is working properly and that it is burning off various slight infections that are formed in the body. Many people who do not vaccinate their children have a sniffle or two until the child is in college and then they would have very few problems. Except they want the chickenpox and they want the measles. So they will have chickenpox parties and measles parties around age five or six.

MO: Yes, I remember. As soon as one of the kids in the neighborhood would get chickenpox, you would literally send the word out and everybody would bring their kids over to be exposed all at one time and be done with it.

GH: And consequently, the virus would usually be mild, with the child being sick for maybe a week, that's it. And that is another test of the immune system because it will burn it off.

MO: I remember that with measles there tended to be a pretty good temperature for a period of time.

GH: But remember also that the fever will burn off not only the measles virus but other viruses as well. The one problem I see with the chickenpox virus is that in the last year, doctors have discovered that juvenile diabetes is due to a virus. They are pretty certain it is the chickenpox virus causing it when suppressed. Once suppressed the virus sets up a new home in the pancreas, thus causing juvenile diabetes.

MO: What is it normally suppressed with?

GH: Normally with drugs to make the child feel better. Fever medications such as Aspirin and Tylenol. That type of thing.

MO: So, once again the driving down of the temperature is the problem because it does not allow the virus to burn off. Would you say that most parents start suppressing the temperature at around one hundred?

GH: Yes, and that is the beginning of the problems. Arthritis has also been shown to be caused by the suppression, as well as Multiple Sclerosis and other autoimmune diseases.

MO: This concept that problems will occur, be suppressed and then rebound later is an interesting one that most people don't see or understand.

GH: Yes. A scenario to be aware of is the length of time a temperature goes on. If the temperature extends more than three days, sometimes the immune response can literally get stuck and a homeopathic like *arnica* can be used to reboot the system. It unsticks the healing response. In children, you could see a difference in as little as fifteen minutes when the healing response becomes unstuck. In adults, it might take two or three hours to reboot the system.

Appendix 3

Meditation and the Braintap Glasses

As I mentioned previously, learning how to quiet your brain is one of the most important skills that your children can learn. As a hypnotherapist, I use Braintap glasses with all of my clients. This light and sound technology gently moves your mind out of the stress levels of beta consciousness and into Theta consciousness within six minutes. With just a little practice clients have been able to move into Theta in less than one minute. My grandchildren have used them for years. Currently, there are more than seven hundred recordings available to use with the glasses. For more information, visit my website at

www.thequantumchildrenbook.com

Appendix 4

A short explanation about different modalities within Alternative and Natural Medicine

- ❖ Essential Oils
- ❖ Acupuncture
- ❖ Energy Medicine
- ❖ Nutritional Health and Healing

Essential Oils

Light in a Bottle

What are Essential Oils?

Plants contain complex and powerful substances known as essential oils. These are aromatic liquids derived from shrubs, flowers, trees, roots, bushes, herbs and seeds. These distinctive components defend plants from insects, harsh environmental conditions and disease. They are also vital for a plant to grow, live, evolve and adapt to its surroundings. Referred to as the essence of the plant, pure essential oils not only protect the plant but also determine its aroma.

Essential oils are highly concentrated and more potent than dried herbs because the distillation process makes them so concentrated. It requires a large volume of plant material to produce small amounts of a distilled essential oil. For example, it takes five thousand lbs. of rose petals to produce one kilo of rose oil. Adding a single drop of peppermint oil to a glass of water has approximately the same concentration as twenty cups of peppermint tea.

In ancient times, sweet-smelling oils were more respected for both medicinal and healing properties than scent, while today the opposite is true. Thus, modern society is ignoring the greatest attribute of essential oils: their health-giving properties.

Many oils, touted as essential oils, are derived with harsh chemicals, diluted, or copied and produced in a lab. Cheap copies bring cheap results and have the potential to be toxic. Therefore, it is imperative to take great care in choosing high-quality essential oils.

How to Use Essential Oils

Western civilization has been very limited in its use and understanding of essential oil. Most Americans think essential oils are only used for aromatherapy, when in fact they can be much more powerful in many other ways.

First Aid Applications

MINOR AILMENTS

Mix essential oil with a carrier oil, like fractionated coconut oil, then apply to skin. Start with small amounts and find what works for you. Carrier oils slow absorption and allow for even application.

Other Considerations:

- If an essential oil feels uncomfortable, immediately apply more carrier oil, not water.

- **ALWAYS HEAVILY DILUTE AND BE CAREFUL WHEN USING** Cinnamon, Clove or Oregano essential oil. These oils may feel very hot on your skin and can cause discomfort or blistering. Avoid use on broken or tender skin. OTHER OILS THAT CAN FEEL UNCOMFORTABLE are Black Pepper, Eucalyptus, Fennel, Ginger, Lemongrass and Peppermint.

- Don't use essential oils in your eyes, ear canal, or on mucous membranes.

- Citrus oils increase sun sensitivity; allow at least twelve hours between application and exposing skin to the sun.

- Oils and water don't mix completely. Keep this in mind when using oils in the bath or adding oils to drinking water.

- Don't use essential oils with plastic bottles for drinking or storage.

Essential Oil Use

You can use essentials oils in three ways: Topically, Internally (drip into an empty gel cap) and with a Diffuser.

For more serious problems, apply every hour or half hour. For pain and digestion remedies you would typically rub the oils right on the spot of discomfort. For oral applications, dilute with coconut oil and rub on gums or teeth or swish around in the mouth, or drop into an empty vegetarian capsule (available at health food stores).

The beauty of the essential oils is that research has consistently proven them to be healthy for our cells. They repair our bodies at a cellular level, so when you are not sure which oils to use, don't be afraid to use several oils and the body will gain a myriad of benefits.

Massage

By adding essential oils to your massage oil base you receive multiple benefits at once. The skin is touched, circulation is increased, and the essential oils are both absorbed and inhaled. For massage, virtually all single oils and blends may be used.

Bath Time

Adding five to ten drops of essential oils to your bath water mixed with Epsom salts or bath gel base is an easy and delightful way to soothe your body and relax. This also produces multiple benefits at once from full-body skin absorption and the aromatic fragrance.

Diffuse Into the Air

Diffusing oils into the air has powerful effects on your environment, your body and your mind. Many oils are known for their abilities to kill germs. A diffuser vaporizes a fine mist of oils into the air. Entire areas can be sterilized. European hospitals have found essential oils more effective at killing infectious agents such as E-coli and Staph than so-called traditional methods using various chemical agents.

Internal Consumption

Research indicates that some oils are more effective when taken orally. Only pure essential oils proven safe and labeled as dietary supplements should be used internally.

Cleaners/Disinfectants

Virtually every household and bathroom cleaning product can be replaced with essential oils. They have powerful, clinically proven antiseptic, antiviral and antifungal properties. Many hospitals in Europe recognize the value of cleaning with Lemon essential oil.

Where to Find Organic Essential Oils

The ability of essential oils to act on both the mind and body is what makes them truly unique. As we begin to understand the true power of essential oils in the realm of personal, holistic healthcare, one must appreciate the necessity for obtaining the purest oils possible.

To order or find out more about organic essential oils, please contact my wife, Allyn Orwig at abreech370@aol.com or visit one of her two websites:

www.buybareoils.com/quantumdoc

www.youngliving.com, member number 238526

Essential Oils desk reference April 2011 Life Science Publishing Printed in the USA

Acupuncture

http://www.miltonacupuncture.net/introduction-to-acupuncture

Traditional Chinese Medicine (TCM) (Daria Casinelli, n.d.)

Acupuncture works by moving the natural energy of your body through twelve channels that connect your internal organs with your body's surface. In ancient China, this energy was called "Qi" (pronounced "chee") and was ascribed many spiritual, emotional and physical powers. If Qi is abundant and flowing smoothly, then an individual enjoys good health. Pain and other physical and emotional disharmonies are the results of Qi being deficient or not flowing smoothly.

There are several different kinds of Qi, and each can be likened to a kind of electricity that travels through the meridian system of the body. Prenatal Qi is the Qi of Destiny. Its mission is to compel us to manifest our genetic and spiritual blueprint and it connects us to the metaphysical world. This is one of the reasons that acupuncture treatments feel so good.

During a treatment, you may feel as if you're having a transcendent experience or as if you are an embryo floating in the primordial womb. This is because when the prenatal Qi is activated you are in touch with the metaphysical world; it is coursing through your body. And, because the meridian system is the communication system of the embryo, during a treatment you are an embryo again, that is nature before nurture. Your body is hearing and implementing its genetic message without interference from all that has passed since birth.

Cloud

A very old interpretation of illness

Imagine your body as cloud made up of gasses instead of liquids. That is trillions of chemical reactions happening all the time. Science has proven that these reactions happen faster in the cells located by acupuncture points. Now imagine that instead of grouping those chemical reactions by the organ in the vicinity of where they happen, you instead divided them into Five Phases. These Five Phases are one of the most basic concepts of TCM. Each phase has a physical and emotional aspect and encompasses hundreds of symptoms that may or may not overlap with Western organ or disease categories.

The Five Phases operate like a circuit, each one leading to the next. The images on this website describe the Five Phases. Understanding the interaction of the phases, especially which Phase is distressed, is the key to diagnosis, especially when practicing Japanese method acupuncture.

The Five Phases of Japanese Method Acupuncture – water The Five Phases of Japanese Method Acupuncture – wood The Five Phases of Japanese Method Acupuncture – fire The Five Phases of Japanese Method Acupuncture – earth The Five Phases of Japanese Method Acupuncture

Energy Channels and Waterways

Qi flows in meridians

The best analogy for the all the communication systems in the body—meridians, circulatory, hormonal, nervous—is that of the Earth's waterways. Water flows through oceans, rivers, swamps, brooks and tiny temporary channels the same way biological information flows through the meridians, nervous system, digestive system etc. The acupuncture meridians, also known as channels, are the most subtle of all the body's waterways, comparable to vernal streams that only appear when full. Filling or draining these channels as necessary is the aim of the acupuncturist.

Like all waterways, our bodies are under the guidance of the moon and susceptible to other natural phenomena. For this reason, your acupuncturist may, particularly for menopausal women, time your treatment with the phases of the moon, or question you closely about how you feel during particular seasons.

242

The Weather

Acupuncture diagnosis and the environment

A traditional Chinese diagnosis is very different from a Western diagnosis. To the untrained ear, it may sound more like a weather report than a medical condition. For instance, your condition may be called "damp" or "stagnant." This is because the ancient Chinese believed that the rules that govern the natural world also govern our bodies. Thus, they described bodily processes in environmental terms. The relationship between your body and the environment is one reason your acupuncturist may prescribe a seasonal tune-up.

The Black Box

Penetrating interview, painless insertion

By inserting sterile, disposable, hair-thin needles into specific points on the body, an acupuncturist regulates the meridians and restores good health. Although the insertions are simple (and painless!) the procedure for choosing the points is not. Your acupuncturist formulates a TCM diagnosis and treatment plan using information gathered during an extensive interview and drawing on years of clinical experience and academic training.

The ancient Chinese were remarkably adept at figuring out what was going on inside the "black box" of their patients' bodies. As their heirs, our most important diagnostic tools are deep listening and careful observation. Today's acupuncture diagnosis is based on what, during an extensive interview, you tell your acupuncturist about your health: the quality, shape, size and speed of your pulse, what the acupuncturist sees when she looks at you and what she feels when she palpates your abdomen.

Asia

A Healing History

Traditional Chinese Medicine, also known at Traditional Asian Medicine, was born in China as herbology and acupuncture. In

China, the categories of herbology were grafted onto the parallel system of acupuncture in a way that doesn't do acupuncture justice, in spite of their common heritage. Both methodologies migrated around Asia and were the dominant healing method for hundreds of years. During the modern era in Japan, Western medicine predominated and included acupuncture. Herbology fell out of favor but acupuncture grew and flourished. As a result, herbology is much more developed in China than in other countries and the acupuncture practiced in Japan has more in common with science than Chinese style acupuncture. This is primarily because of the work of Yoshio Manaka, MD. Moxa

Increasing Effectiveness of Acupuncture

Moxa is one of several adjunct modalities that help make an acupuncture treatment more effective. Moxa wool, made of dried Mugwort leaves (Artemisia Vulgaris) is burned either above the skin, on the head of the needle, or directly on the skin over a layer of ointment. When burned, moxa produces an intense dry heat that moves your Qi and warms your body. Moxa is especially useful if you always feel cold or if your condition worsens in cold weather.

Waking Up

What happens during a treatment

There are over four hundred known acupuncture points, each with its own unique effect on Qi and overall health. The most frequently used points are located below the knees and elbows. When the needles are inserted most patients feel a very small pinch, less than a mosquito bite, followed by a sensation of warmth or heaviness. That sensation is the Qi waking up and traveling through the channels to the affected area. Once the needles are inserted they remain in place for ten to thirty minutes. During this time, most patients are pleased to find that they become deeply relaxed.

Modernity

Scientists discover

Compelled by the positive results experienced by thousands of patients, modern science is coming closer to defining Qi as a pathway where chemical reactions occur faster than in other parts of the body. Ask your acupuncturist for copies of articles describing how magnetic resonance imagining (MRI) has traced the path of Qi. Or better yet, come in and experience it yourself. More Information

Energy Medicine

What is Energy Medicine? *(Eden, n.d.)*

http://innersource.net/em/about/energy-medicine.html

By Donna Eden

"Energy Medicine brings you vitality when you are drained, health when you are ill, and joy when you are down."

Donna Eden

Energy Medicine awakens energies that bring resilience, joy and enthusiasm to your life—and greater vitality to your body, mind and spirit! Balancing your energies balances your body's chemistry; regulates your hormones, helps you feel better and helps you think better. It has been called the self-care and development path of the future, but it empowers you NOW to adapt to the challenges of the 21st century and to thrive within them.

"In every culture and in every medical tradition before ours, healing was accomplished by moving energy."

Albert Szent-Gyorgyi, MD
Nobel Laureate in Medicine

Energy Medicine Definitions:

Right Brain Definition: "Energy is your body's magic! It is your life force. You keep it healthy and it keeps you healthy. If you are sick or sad, shifting your energies feels good. When you care for these invisible energies, it makes your heart sing and your cells happy!

Donna Eden

246

Left Brain Definition: "Conventional medicine, at its foundation, focuses on the biochemistry of cells, tissue, and organs. Energy Medicine, at its foundation, focuses on the energy fields of the body that organize and control the growth and repair of cells, tissue and organs. Changing impaired energy patterns may be the most efficient, least invasive way to improve the vitality of organs, cells and psyche."

David Feinstein, PhD

Top 4 Questions about Energy Medicine

1. How is Energy Medicine Practiced?

Energy medicine utilizes techniques from time-honored traditions such as acupuncture, yoga, kinesiology, and qi gong. Flow, balance, and harmony can be non-invasively restored and maintained within an energy system by tapping, massaging, pinching, twisting, or connecting specific energy points (acupoints) on the skin; by tracing or swirling the hand over the skin along specific energy pathways; through exercises or postures designed for specific energetic effects; by focusing use of the mind to move specific energies; and/or by surrounding an area with healing energies.

2. How does it Work?

Energy Medicine recognizes energy as a vital, living, moving force that determines much about health and happiness.

The body needs its energies to:

- Move and have space to continue to move—energies may become blocked due to toxins, muscular or other constriction, prolonged stress, or interference from other energies.

- Move in specific patterns—generally in harmony with the physical structures and functions that the energies animate and support. "Flow follows function."

- Crossover—at all levels, from the micro-level of the double helix of DNA, extending to the macro-level where the left side of the brain controls the right side of the body and the right side controls the left.

- Maintain a balance with other energies—the energies may lose their natural balance due to prolonged stress or other conditions that keep specific energy systems in a survival mode.

- Conversely, when the body is not healthy, corresponding disturbances in its energies can be identified and treated.

3. Is Energy Medicine Spiritual?

Entering the world of your body's subtle energies is a bridge into the domain of your deepest spiritual callings and your eternal essence. While no particular belief system, allegiance, or religious affiliation is associated with Energy Medicine, many people find that energy work touches into the realms of soul and spirit.

4. Can Anyone Do it?

Absolutely! Working with your energies is your birthright!

Students of Energy Medicine include:

- Ordinary people with no experience in self-healing or healing others

- Anyone who wants to learn to engage their energies for health and vitality

- People who want to study techniques to help themselves, their family, or a close friend

- Massage therapists, nurses, acupuncturists, doctors, and others in existing healthcare careers who are looking to supplement and enhance their training

- Healthcare professionals looking for courses that offer professional CEs

- People of all ages and all walks of life who want to embark on a career in Energy Medicine

Nutritional Health and Healing

We will be talking more about nutrition in the next book but I still wanted to reinforce how it forms the foundation of every aspect of your health. You cannot own your health and your reality that you are creating when you ignore what you eat and drink. There are so many toxins in our society today it is beyond belief. In essence, every man, woman and child is being poisoned on a daily basis and we wonder why the health in this country is so poor?

So what are your excuses? Everybody has them.

Let's see…we have
- My schedule is too demanding
- My kids are picky eaters
- Health food is too expensive
- I don't have time to cook
- It's too hard

Kid Smart by Cheryl Townsley is an excellent book on nutrition and all that that includes for the family.

Here is a little clip from her book (Townsley, 1996)

"It has long been recognized that the eating patterns and the foods to which children are exposed in the early years of life are among the most influential factors determining their nutritional health as adults." – The Children Nutritional Advisory Council

Parents determine the health of their children from as early as the time of conception. The health of the parents at the time the child is conceived critically impacts the health of the fetus and newborn baby. From as early as birth, children eat the food their parents give them, whether it is breastmilk or formula. Children learn to adopt the eating patterns of their parents. During the formative years of an infant, toddler, and school-age, children are dependent upon their parents for their food, housing, and emotional support.

Are the attitude, knowledge, and action of a parent important to the health of a child? Obviously, yes! Yet, today many American parents are ignoring the blinking yellow lights of sickness and disease in our children's generation. What is the overall health picture of today's average child? It's not as rosy as we'd like to believe."

> One in six children is seriously deficient in calcium.

    (Needed for strong bones and teeth)

> One in three children is deficient in iron.

    (Needed for energy, immune system and attention span)

> Nearly one in two children is deficient in zinc.

    (Needed for immune function, skin, healthy sexual development, wound healing, overall growth and blood pressure regulation)

> Nearly three million children between the ages of six and seventeen years suffer from high blood pressure.

> The list goes on and on.

    – Summarized from the Vitamin Supplement Journal

> Beyond these deficiencies, 60 percent of American children are overweight according to the American Heart Association

The National Cancer Institute's research indicates that children between grades two and six have the following beliefs about nutrition:

> 15% believe cheese is a good source of fiber (it isn't)
> 48% believe apple juice has more fat than whole milk (it doesn't)
> 36% believe watermelon has more fat than American cheese (it doesn't)

251

Summary of Where to Start

Kid Smart devotes a whole chapter to this subject to explain these fully:

- Step one:　make a decision
- Step two:　get in unity
- Step three: include your children
- Step four:　examine your food traditions
- Step five:　identify the cost of change
- Step six:　establish the price you are willing to pay
- Step seven: develop an attitude
- Step eight: begin to ADD:
  - more fruits and vegetables
  - more organic
  - more whole grains, beans, raw nuts, seeds and sprouts
  - more pure water
  - supplementation
- Step nine: begin to SUBTRACT:
  - minimize food processed with chemicals
  - minimize food with hydrogenated fat products
  - Minimize the "whites"
  - minimize meats with chemicals
  - minimize dairy products
  - minimize canned foods
- Step 10: learn alternatives
- Step 11: have incentives
- Step 12: rejoice

The Importance of Eating Organic

This is an article from Dr. Mercola's website that will give you an

excellent place to start your ADDs and SUBTRACTS.

The "Dirty Dozen" Fruits and Vegetables
Containing the Most Pesticides

November 28, 2006

The Environmental Working Group (EWG) has produced a new wallet-size Shoppers' Guide listing the twelve fruits and vegetables that are the most contaminated with pesticides (the "Dirty Dozen"), as well as those that generally contain the lowest amount of pesticides (the "Cleanest Twelve").

The information is based on nearly forty three thousand tests conducted by the USDA and FDA.

The last EWG Guide was issued in 2015.

An analysis by the EWG estimated that consumers could reduce their exposure to pesticides by almost ninety percent merely by avoiding foods on their "Dirty Dozen" list. Here is the updated 2015 list:

1. Apples
2. Peaches
3. Nectarines
4. Strawberries
5. Grapes
6. Celery
7. Spinach
8. Sweet bell peppers
9. Cucumbers
10. Cherry tomatoes
11. Snap peas—imported
12. Potatoes

Conversely, the "Cleanest Twelve," according to the EWG, only exposes you to fewer than two pesticides per day, a huge difference from the fifteen pesticides per day you'd be exposed to with the fruits and vegetables on the "Dirty Dozen" list. Among the cleanest fruits and vegetables you can buy at your grocery store:

1. Avocado
2. Sweet Corn
3. Pineapple
4. Cabbage
5. Sweet peas (frozen)
6. Onions
7. Asparagus
8. Mangos
9. Papayas
10. Kiwi
11. Eggplant
12. Grapefruit
13. Cantaloupe
14. Cauliflower
15. Sweet Potatoes

Dr. Mercola's Comments:

Remember that the Environmental Protection Agency (EPA) considers sixty percent of herbicides, ninety percent of fungicides and thirty percent of insecticides to be carcinogenic.

Pesticides can have many negative influences on health, including neurotoxicity, disruption of the endocrine system, and carcinogenicity and immune system suppression. Pesticide exposure may also affect male reproductive function and has been linked to miscarriages in women.

That's just part of the reason why you should always be on the lookout for organically grown fruits and vegetables. Where traditional farmers apply chemical fertilizers to the soil to grow their crops, organic farmers feed and build soil with natural fertilizer.

Traditional farmers use insecticides to get rid of insects and disease, while organic farmers use natural methods such as insect predators and barriers for this purpose. Traditional farmers control weed growth by applying synthetic herbicides, but organic farmers use crop rotation, tillage, hand weeding, cover crops and mulches to control weeds.

The result is that organically grown food is not tainted with chemical residues, which can be harmful to humans.

The major problem most people have with organic food is the expense.

However, if you plan wisely, eating organically is actually quite affordable. A diet based on whole organic foods does not have to be **cost-prohibitive for the average family or single consumer**.

However, I'd like to say that if the choice is between fresh conventional vegetables and wilted organic ones, I would recommend you choose the conventional vegetables; old and wilted vegetables lose many of the vital micronutrients that make them so healthy. If you do buy conventional vegetables, I certainly recommend that you go with the ones on the "Cleanest Twelve" list.

Appendix 5
Kinesiology

How to tune within for answers to your questions takes on many forms. I first was exposed to kinesiology by a mentor of mine, Sandra Michael. She was an amazing healer and had worked with supplements decades before they became popular. We tested every supplement I had to see what my body actually resonated with. Out of twenty over-the-counter supplements that I used at different times, only two proved beneficial to my body.

The style of testing we used required two people, a tester and a subject. Here is a YouTube clip showing this style.

Troy Giles - Applied Kinesiology Introduction
https://youtu.be/VoSffSLBX3A

Troy does an excellent job explaining and demonstrating kinesiology in this clip. In this example, we have a practitioner and a patient. What if you are by yourself?

Cynthia Sue Larson - Learn How to Muscle Test Yourself in 3 Minutes
https://youtu.be/5M8WbR-dOfY

Scott Gamble - How to Self–Muscle test for Truth
https://youtu.be/zTJKxjzqsnM

Holly Worton - How to Do Self Muscle Testing ~ 7 Ways to Muscle Test Yourself
https://youtu.be/c9ikRMlI-jY

Dev Khalsa - Using Kinesiology to Access Your Heart Intelligence
https://youtu.be/GHj2zdWzcec

I studied kinesiology in workshops where I could practice and ask questions in a learning environment. I think this is still the best method. I also studied how to dowse using a pendulum. Eventually, you should get to the point where you simply feel the answers within. All of these techniques are tools to help you reach this point. There are nuances involved with these practices and your job is to learn what works best for you.

Bibliography

Achor, S. (2010). *The Happiness Advantage*. Crown Publishing.

Bartholomew, A. (2002). *The Schauberger Keys*. Wellow, Bath, UK: Sulis Health.

Bartholomew, A. (2010). *The Spiritual Life of Water*. Rochester, VT, USA: Park Street Press.

Bigelsen, H. (2007). *Holographic Blood*. San Francisco, CA, USA: Harvey Bigelsen, Inc.

Collins, M. (n.d.). *What is herbology? Retrieved from www.allthinshealing.com: http://www.allthingshealing.com/what-is-herbology.php#.VwKhJPkrLcs*

Daria Casinelli, L. A. (n.d.). *Introduction to Acupuncture. Retrieved from www.miltonacupuncture.net: http://www.miltonacupuncture.net/introduction-to-acupuncture*

Dickerson, I. (2013, January 16). *Earth Breathing. Retrieved July 3, 2014, from Earth Breathing: http/:wwwearthbreathing.co.uk.sr.htm*

Dr. Paul Drouin of Quantum University. (2010, December 1). *Five Pillars Of Health. Five Pillars of Health*. Honolulu, HI, USA: Quantum University.

Dweck, C. (n.d.). *Retrieved from mindsetworks.com: http://www.mindsetworks.com/*

Eden, D. (n.d.). *Eden Energy Medicine. Retrieved from innersource.net: http://innersource.net/em/about/energy-medicine.html*

Edgar Cayce, T. K. (n.d.). *Akashic Records - The Book of Life. Retrieved from Edgar Cayce's A. R. E: http://www.edgarcayce.org/are/spiritualGrowth.aspx?id=2078*

Emoto, M. (n.d.). *Messages from Water*. Hado Publishing.

Frazer, S. J. (1922). *The Golden Bough*. New York: Macmillan.

Garrison, C. (2004). *Slim Spurling's Universe*. Frederick, CO, USA: IX-EL Publishing LLC.

Gerber, R. (2000). *Vibrational Medicine for the 21st Century*. New York, NY, USA: HarperCollins Publishers, Inc.

Goswami, A. (2004). *The Quantum Doctor*. Charlottesville, VA, USA: Hampton Roads Publishing Company, Inc.

Haras, S. (n.d.). *sarahharas07*. Retrieved from deviantart.com: http://sarahharas07.deviantart.com/

Health, F. N. (2012, 05 02). *How can chiropractors benefit your health?* Retrieved from www.foxnews.com: http://www.foxnews.com/health/2012/05/02/how-can-chiropractors-benefit-your-health.html

Hicks, E. a. (2004). *Ask and it is Given*. Hay House.

Higgins, M. B. (1973). *Wilhem Reich a Cancer Biopathy*. Toronto , Ontario, Canada: Doubleday.

Hoffman, G. (2009, December 03). *Boulder, CO*.

Holst, U. (2004). *The Healing Power of Energized Water*. Rochester, VT, USA: Healing Arts Press.

Holst, U. (2010). *The Healing Power of Energized Water*. Rochester , VT, USA: Healing Arts Press.

Last, W. (2009, June 15). *Bioenergies*. Retrieved February 10, 2012, from Health Science Spirit : http://www.health-science-spirit.com

Last, W. (2010, February 12). *Living Water*. Retrieved April 30, 2012, from Health Science Spirit: http://www.health-science-spirit.com

Lipton, B. (2008). *The Biology of Belief*. New York, NY, USA: Hay House .

McTaggart, L. (2007). *The Intention Experiment*. New York, NY, USA: Free Press.

McTaggart, L. (2008). *The Field*. New York, NY, USA: Harper Collins.

Mercola, D. (2006, November 28). *The Dirty Dozen Fruits and Vegetables Containing the Most Pesticides.* Retrieved from www.mercola.com: http://articles.mercola.com/sites/articles/archive/2006/11/28/the-dirty-dozen-fruits-and-vegetables-containing-the-most-pesticides.aspx

Mercola, D. (2010, November 03). *Hepatitis B Vaccine: Refuse This Routine Procedure – Or Expose Your Baby's Brain to Severe Danger.* Retrieved from drmercola.com: http://articles.mercola.com/sites/articles/archive/2010/11/03/hepatitis-b-vaccines-at-birth.aspx

Mercola, D. (2012, 05 12). *Fermented Foods Contain 100 TIMES More Probiotics than a Supplement.* Retrieved from www.mercola.com: http://articles.mercola.com/sites/articles/archive/2012/05/12/dr-campbell-mcbride-on-gaps.aspx

Michaels, L. (n.d.). (M. Orwig, Interviewer)

Michaels, L. (2005).

Michaels, L. (2014).

Michaels, L. (2016). (M. Orwig, Interviewer)

MJ Pangman, a. M. (2011). *Dancing with Water.* Denver, CO, USA: Uplifting Press.

Nutri-Science, D. F. (2013, June 1). *Native American Nutri-Science.* Retrieved June 15, 2014, from Native American Nutri-Science Escozine: www.nativeamericannutriscience.com

Oschman, J. L. (2000). *Energy Medicine The Scientific Basis.* London, England: Churchhill Livingstone.

Paths, L. (n.d.). *Life Paths.* Retrieved from wolfsmoon.tripod.com: http://wolfsmoon.tripod.com/whitetigertotem.html

Popova, A. (Director). (2008). *Water The Great Mystery* [Motion Picture]. Russia.

Publishing, L. S. (2011). *Essential Oils desk reference.* Life Science Publishing.

Schwenk, T. (1989). *Water The Element of Life.* Hudson, NY, USA: Anthroposophic Press Inc.

Tennant, D. J. (2016, April). *Electric Health with Dr. Jerry Tennant.* (R. Meredith, Interviewer)

The Living Matrix (2009). *[Motion Picture].*

Tooley, A. C. (1997, January 15). *Vibrational Healing.* Retrieved September 21, 2012, from http//www.luminati.com: http//www.luminati.com

Townsley, C. (1996). *Kid Smart. In C. Townsley, Kid Smart* (pp. 20, 29, 53).

Ullman, D. (1987). *Homeopathy: Medicine for the 21st Century.*

Ullman, D. (n.d.). *A condensed history of homeopathy.* Retrieved from www.homeopathic.com: https://www.homeopathic.com/Articles/Introduction_to_Homeopathy/A_Condensed_History_of_Homeopathy.html

Yury Kronn, P. (2010, March 15). *Understanding the Secrets of Subtle Energy.* (D. P. Drouin, Interviewer)

CPSIA information can be obtained
at www.ICGtesting.com
Printed in the USA
FSOW03n0216020617
34678FS